I0161816

Coloring Light

Illuminated Bible Verses

27 Luminaries to Color

Corinne Shibley

© 2016 Corinne M. Shibley. Permission is granted to the purchaser of this book to photocopy the designs only for personal coloring use, not for distribution. All rights reserved.

Unless otherwise noted, all Scripture taken from the New King James Version.
Copyright © 1982 by Thomas Nelson, Inc.
Used by permission. All rights reserved.

Scripture quotation marked ESV is from The Holy Bible, English Standard Version, copyright © 2001 by Crossway Bibles, a division of Good News Publishers.
Used by permission, all rights reserved.

Stained glass elements are from Franz Meyer of Munich windows at 8000 Brook Road, Richmond, Virginia

ISBN: 978-0-692-61438-9
This book is available from Amazon.com, CreateSpace.com and other retail outlets.

A Publication of HGBG Productions
coloringlight.com

God created a world of color. Sometimes that color is bold and saturated, sometimes it's quiet and subdued. Without light there is no color, only darkness. Color these simple paper luminary designs and add light to a dark corner or to brighten someone's day.

Lovers of classic old black and white movies, and, more recently, the art of Zentangle® are drawn to the beauty and amazing visual depth that can be achieved with shades of black and white. As an art student, I was taught to create in black and white before being allowed to move to color. I was impatient to use color, a more natural expression of the world around me, but the lessons I learned working in shades of gray were invaluable.

I present my designs to color along with tips and observations for everyone who likes the relaxation of coloring without the challenge of drawing. Starting from a blank page is intimidating, even to experienced artists.

Showing your coloring talent by adding light is easy with some very simple cutting and pasting. Let your colors shine!

CAUTION: these luminaries are not to be used with an open flame or heat producing bulbs.

MATERIALS NEEDED
In addition to this book:

- colored pencils and pens or markers

- scissors

- Duck brand peel & stick clear laminate or
  clear Contact paper (optional and highly recommended)

- white glue (quick setting is best) or glue stick for paper
  For laminated luminaries, Goop all purpose adhesive

- LED lights (stick on puck lights)

CONTRAST

CONTRAST, the difference in lightness and darkness, is an important consideration when coloring. The starkest contrast will always be black and white. Midtones are the many grays that are somewhere between black and white, some of them can be seen below. The deep grays that are close to black, offer little contrast to black. Similarly, the lightest grays that are closest to white, offer little contrast to white.

The eye is always drawn to the sharp contrast of black (no light) and white (the most light). Values of gray are fairly easily distinguished, Alas, the world is not black and white. Sometimes it is helpful when deciding on color to look at the colors when the color is really not obvious, as in low light levels, or through squinted eyes. Colors with little contrast will be almost indistinguishable from each other. A good balance of contrast provides interest without making the eyes weary as can happen when there are multiple sharp contrasts without midtones. The eye has difficulty focusing without contrast. Contrast can sometimes be more easily seen by adjusting colored pictures to black and white on the computer, as shown in the samples below.

All of the samples above were colored with the same colors. The one on the left was colored with light values using colored pencils, the one in the middle was colored with dark colors using colored pens. The sample on the right was colored in both dark and light versions of the same colors, the darker tones colored with pens, and the lighter tones colored with pencils. The computer stripped the colors away, leaving black and white with shades of gray. The one that combined both light and dark, pencils and pens has more contrast, the details are easier to see with less eye strain.

ADDING 3D effects to 2D shapes makes objects appear to pop off the page. The circles in the first 3 samples below were colored in completely or left uncolored, and remain flatly 2 dimensional. The next 3 samples added shading to the circles, making the circles appear to be spheres. The spheres on the left appear to be floating in space. By adding shadows, the middle spheres are grounded to the gray background. The spheres on the right have been transformed to the recognizable shape of a baseball, and the shadows indicate they are not in flight.

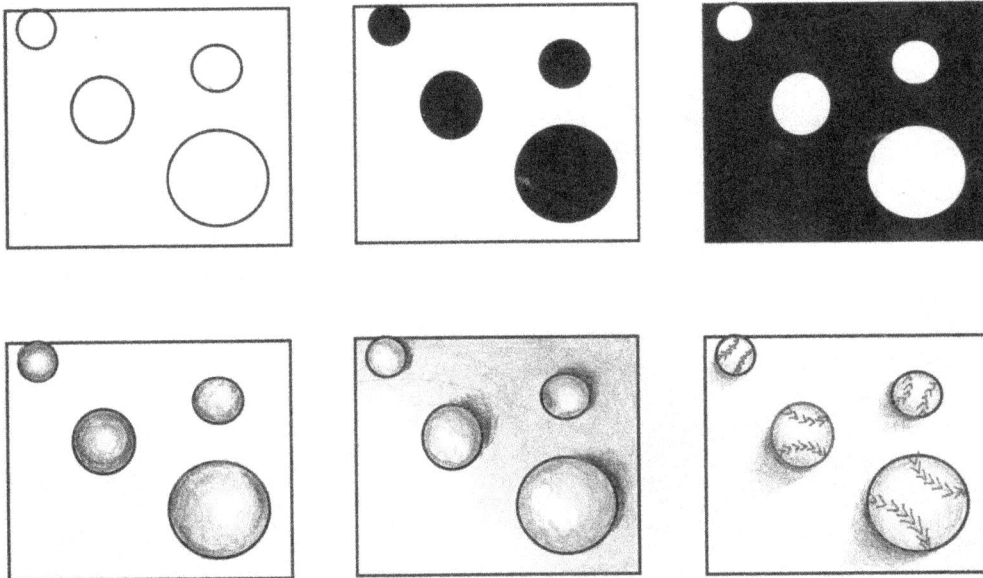

Shading from light to dark within a shape is what makes it look 3D. The 2 circles on the far left of the second row above don't quite look 3D because the shading is done very regularly, the dark and medium values form even rings and the lightest value is in the center. The darkest part of a sphere is around the outside edge, the medium is within the dark, and the lightest within the medium. That said, there should be no well defined transition from dark to medium to light, and the light should be off center.

The samples below of a ribbon like shape show light coming from different angles. The one on the left has light from directly above, and is 2D. The ribbon shape could be a curvy river on a map. The light comes in from the left on the ribbon shape in the middle, with the light hitting the closest parts of the ribbon. The light comes in from the right on the far right sample. Play with light as you color, modeling shapes either realistically or fancifully. It's really fun to watch shapes change from 2D to 3D.

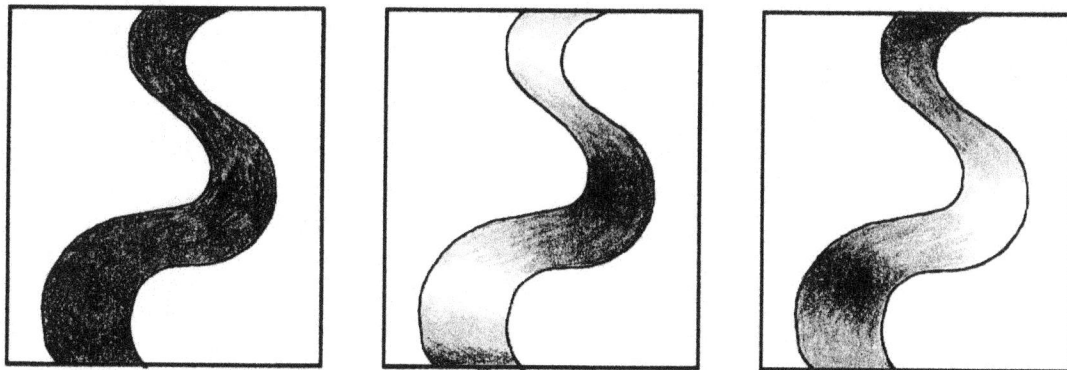

SHADOWS occur outside a shape, and can be more colors than gray. While they have a

harder edge right next to the object casting the shadow, the shadow dissolves as it moves away from the object. Shadows can be long or short, hard or soft, and they are can be on one or two sides of the shape, depending on the angle of the light. Shadows can be cast from two perpendicular sides. Realistically, the shadows formed are seldom the same distance from both sides.

LISTEN TO YOUR EYES. Sherlock Holmes is always telling Dr. Watson that he sees

but does not observe. Selective seeing is pretty routine in our cluttered lives. In order to color successfully, it's helpful to process more of the information that comes through our eyes. Try to observe closely the way light changes the way color is seen, especially around the edges and where the light hits the parts closest to the light source.

COLOR THEORY

COLOR THEORY is a rather cumbersome set of formulas that can be a hindrance as much as a help. Color is often a personal preference that goes beyond a formula. A beginning colorist would do well to remember the basic identification of colors on the colorwheel with the acronym Roy G. Biv. Like a cat chasing its tail, red is the cat's nose, and Violet (purple) is the tip of his tail, and they sit side by side on the color wheel.

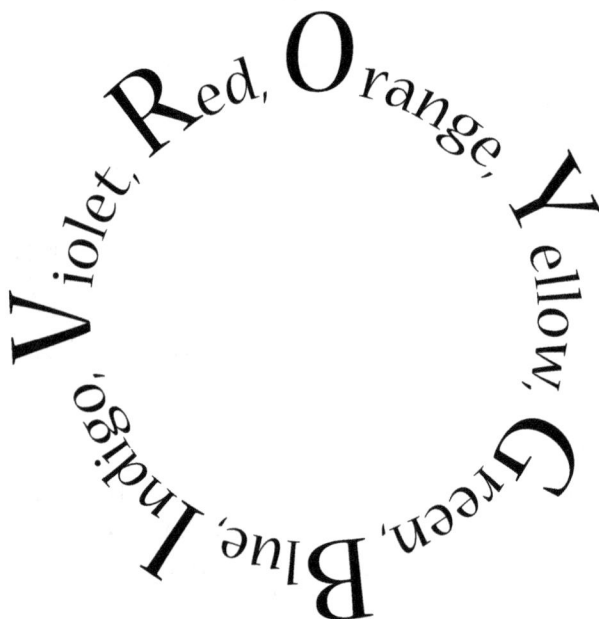

Violet, Red, Orange, Yellow, Green, Blue, Indigo,

Every color fits somewhere on the wheel. There are many colors between any 2 colors on the color wheel. It's not necessary to know the exact location of a color. Knowing that turquoise fits somewhere between blue and green is enough. Browns can be dark yellow, dark orange, or dark red, or anywhere between the 3.

Safe color combinations can always be found next to each other on the color wheel. Pick any color, say violet (purple) as a starting point for picking colors. You could move clockwise around the color wheel, including red, orange and yellow. You could also move counterclockwise around the wheel, choosing indigo, blue and green to go with the violet. I like to think of indigo as navy blue, the blue on the color wheel is much brighter blue, closer to ultramarine.

How color is distributed is as important as what color it is. A big, bold red shape can be complemented by a smaller, different shape of the same red. When using multiple colors, it's usually best to distribute them fairly evenly throughout the picture.

COLORED PENCILS

COLORED PENCILS are made of wax, and are somewhat like crayons. Pencils that take a fine point can color the tiniest details. There are blending pens and pencils available, and blending can also be done by the application of a lighter color such as white over the color to be blended, which changes the color and can sometimes look hazy. The color sits on the surface of the paper without being absorbed. There is a limit to how much wax the paper will hold.

The colors that pencils come in may seem limited, but they can be layered together to produce the between colors that don't come in the set. Both expensive and cheaper pencils can be used. I mix them freely for a wider range of colors. Pencils can also be bought one at a time to add more options. I haven't come across pencils I won't use. The more expensive pencils have more wax, the cheaper ones are more chalky which makes them easier to blend.

Blow, don't wipe unwanted bits of colors from the surface of the paper.

Practice zero pressure. Zero pressure means the hand holding the pencil simply moves the pencil over the paper with no downward pressure, leaving the lightest trace of color possible. This is vital to feathering colors to blend them seamlessly or to create shadows and highlights. I have seen complaints about less expensive pencils breaking. With zero pressure, even the softest points don't break.

Always start light, with a light layer of both wax and color You can always go darker (by gradually adding more pressure), as long as there isn't a heavy layer of wax that won't accept anymore color. Going from dark to light just isn't going to happen.

COLORED PENS or markers are a great way to add vibrant color. The ink is absorbed by the paper. Anywhere the tip of the pen rests on the paper, a blob of ink will be absorbed. Pressure isn't needed to apply color. Practice starting and stopping coloring with pens by using a very light gliding motion, so that the pen is already moving when it first comes into contact with the paper, and lifts off the paper while it is still in motion. It's not really possible to create light values of color with pens or markers, but used with colored pencils, it's easy to get a full range of light and dark.

Before Coloring

BEFORE COLORING either remove the pages from the book or copy them. They may be copied for your own personal coloring use, not for distribution. It's best to color on a hard surface so there won't be any bleeding through to the next page or unwanted impressions from the pressure of a pencil point.

After Coloring

AFTER COLORING laminate, cut the luminaries out, score and glue them as follows.

Laminate first (optional) on both sides of all pieces. See last
page of book for helpful hints to make it easy. Laminated luminaries are much sturdier and your coloring will be protected. Duck brand laminate is acid free.

Cut around the tabs. The gray glue tabs are at the bottom. The white glue
tabs are at the top and the sides. For the white tabs, cut just inside the printed line so the line doesn't show. The edges where there is no tab, just a dotted line, cut on the dotted line.

Cut out the top (if there is one, again cutting off the lines) and bottom for the luminary. Cut out the circle on the bottom to fit over the LED light.

Score and fold dotted lines (except on the sides without tabs)
using a knitting or tapestry needle, and a straight edge. If the dotted lines are hard to see, score between the tabs from top to bottom. Unfold to glue.

Glue the side tabs one at a time, using a small amount of glue, and spreading
it evenly to attach the sides of the luminary first. From the inside, on a hard surface, run a finger along the glue lines to make them smooth and even.

Glue the top to the top front tab first. With the luminary upside down, spread glue on the remaining 3 sides of the top and carefully position over tabs. Smooth from inside.

Glue the bottom to the bottom front tab first. With the luminary right side up, spread glue on the remaining 3 sides of the bottom and carefully position over tabs. Smooth from inside, through hole.

I am Alpha and Omega,

the first and the last.

Revelation 22:13 KJV

the beginning and the end,

© copyright 2016 Corinne M. Shibley. HGBG Productions. All rights reserved.

CAUTION: these luminaries are not to be used with an open flame or heat producing bulbs.

www.coloringlight.com

Luminary Bottom
Cut and remove this
circle for light.

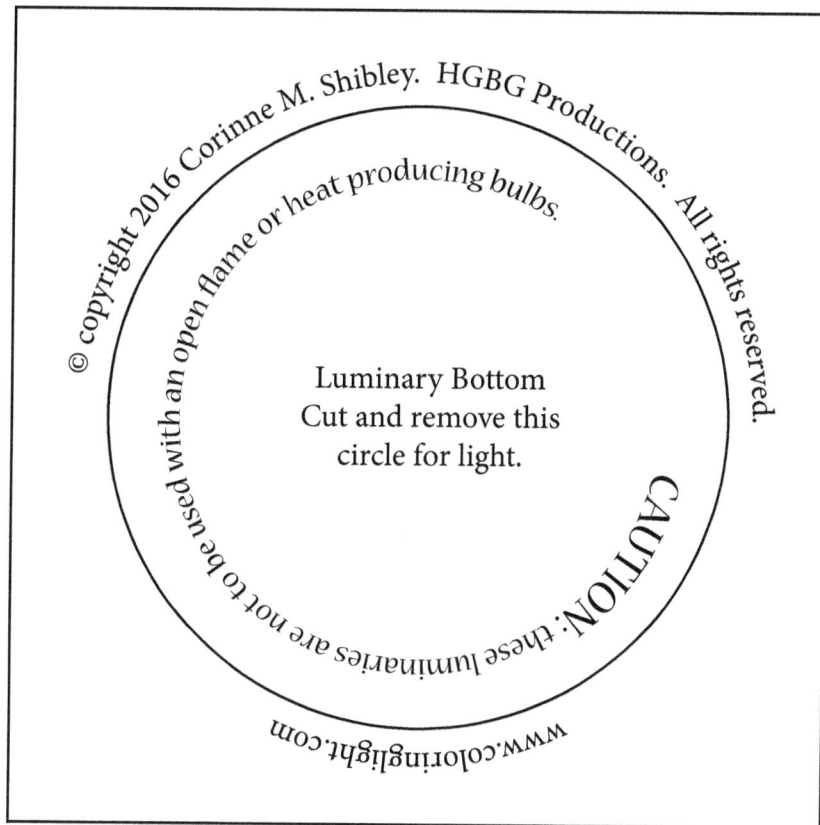

Luminary Top, cut just inside of lines

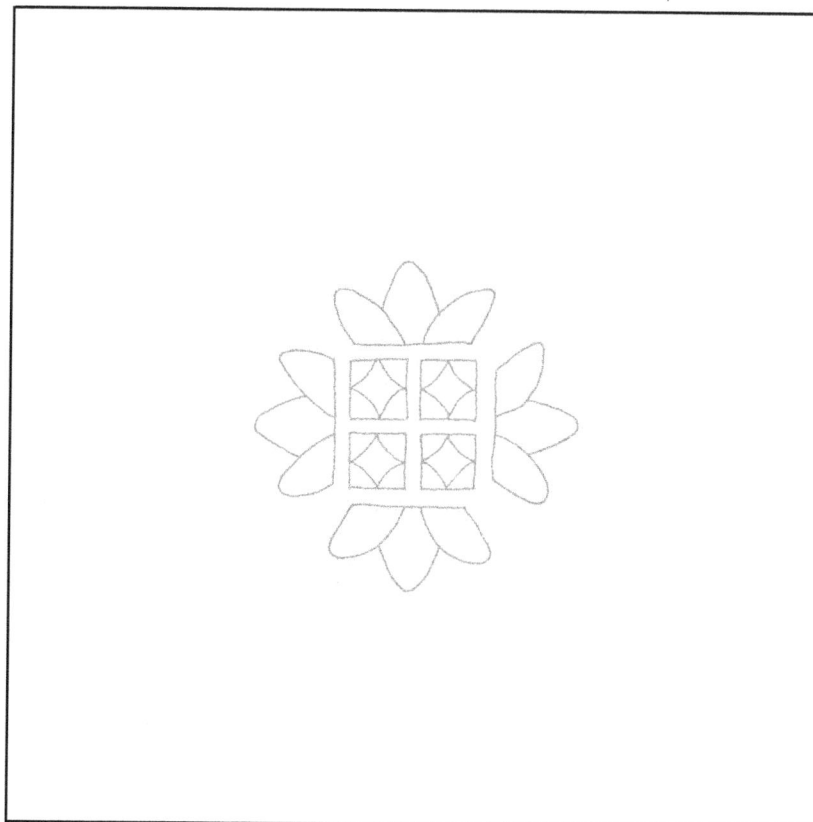

or by grace
you have been
saved through faith,

and that not of yourselves:

lest anyone should boast.
Ephesians 2:8-9

it is the gift of God, not of works

Luminary Bottom
Cut and remove this
circle for light.

© copyright 2016 Corinne M. Shibley. HGBG Productions. All rights reserved.

CAUTION: these luminaries are not to be used with an open flame or heat producing bulbs.

www.coloringlight.com

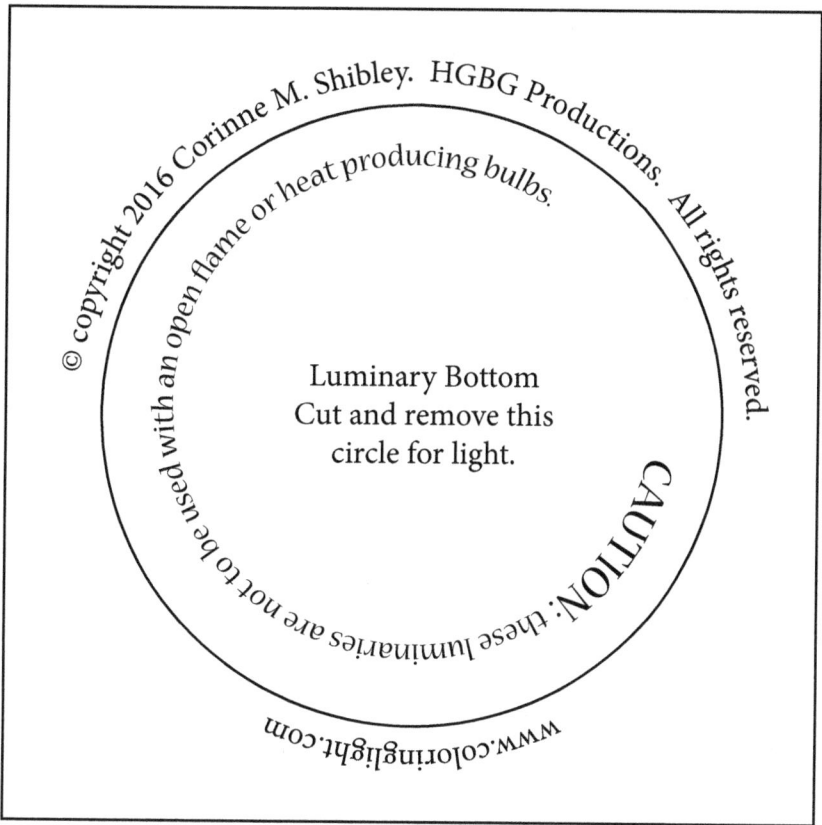

Luminary Top, cut just inside of lines

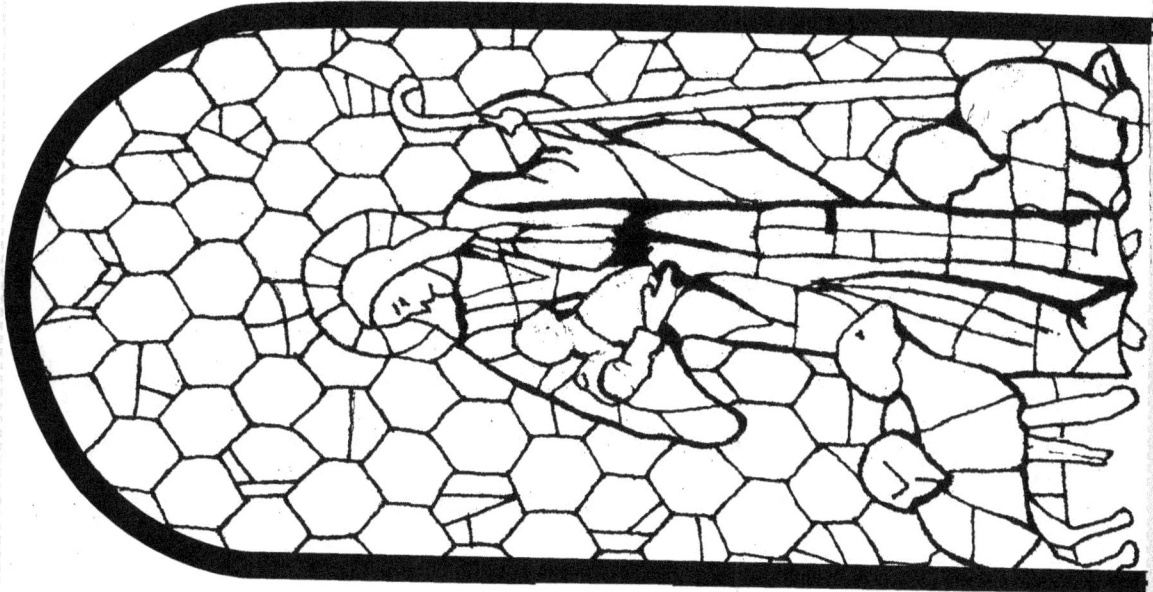

The LORD is my shepherd; I shall not want.

He maketh me to lie down in green pastures: he leadeth me beside the still waters.

He restoreth my soul: he leadeth me in the paths of righteousness for his name's sake.

Yea, though I walk through the valley of the shadow of death, I will fear no evil: for thou art with me; thy rod and thy staff they comfort me.

Thou preparest a table before me in the presence of mine enemies: thou anointest my head with oil; my cup runneth over.

Surely goodness and mercy shall follow me all the days of my life: and I will dwell in the house of the LORD for ever.

Psalm 23 KJV

Luminary Bottom
Cut and remove this
circle for light.

© copyright 2016 Corinne M. Shibley. HGBG Productions. All rights reserved.

CAUTION: these luminaries are not to be used with an open flame or heat producing bulbs.

www.coloringlight.com

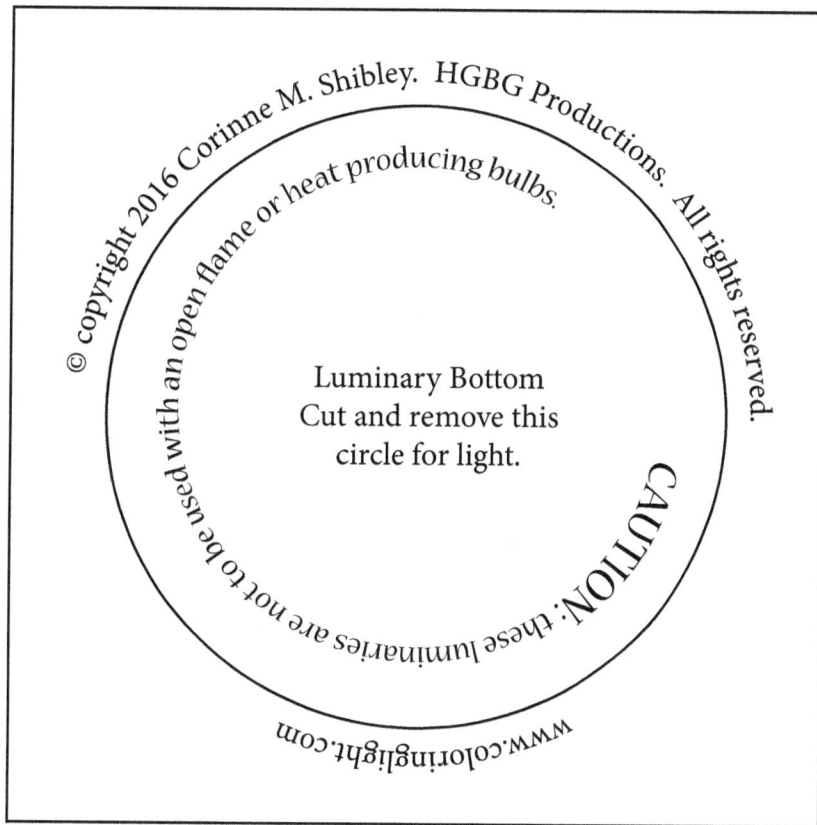

Luminary Top, cut just inside of lines

clear as crystal, proceeding from the throne

nd he showed me a pure river of water of life,

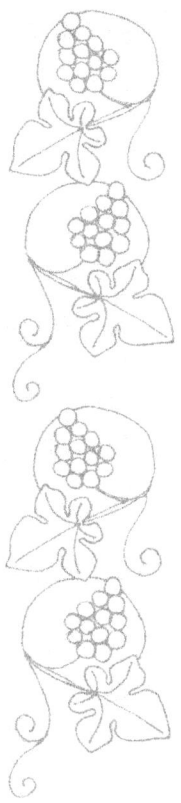

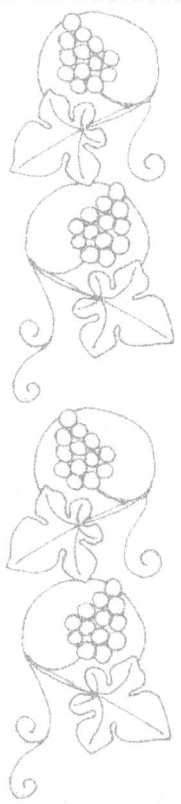

of God and of the Lamb.
Revelation 22:1

Luminary Bottom
Cut and remove this
circle for light.

© copyright 2016 Corinne M. Shibley. HGBG Productions. All rights reserved.

CAUTION: these luminaries are not to be used with an open flame or heat producing bulbs.

www.coloringlight.com

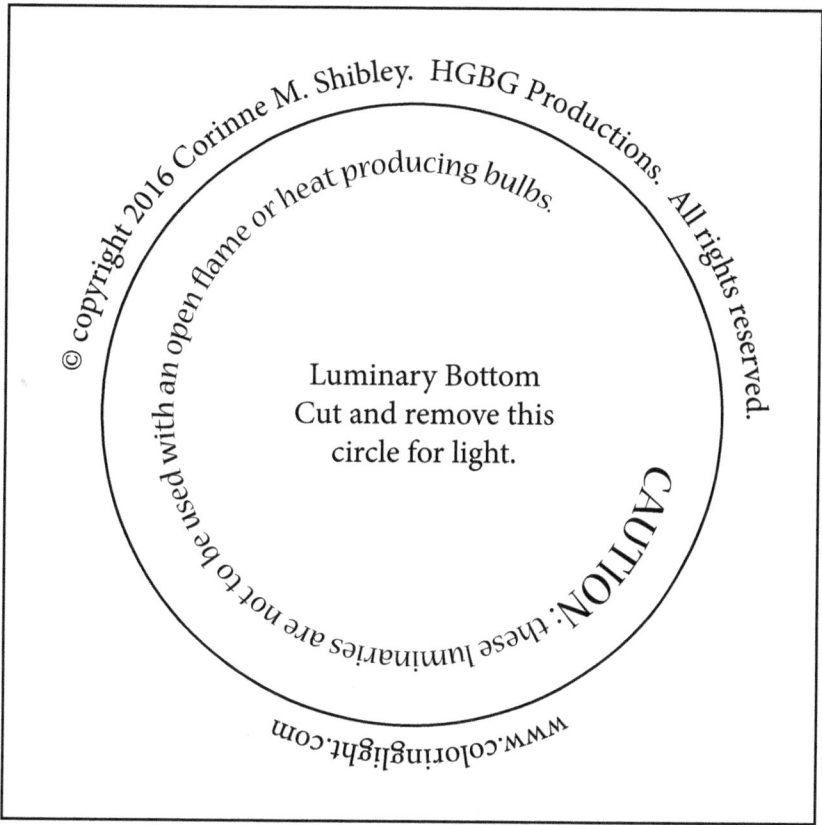

Luminary Top, cut just inside of lines

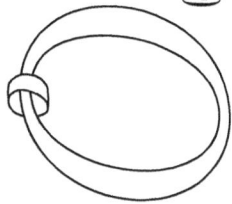

O God,
You know my foolishness;
And my sins are not hidden from You.
Psalm 69:5

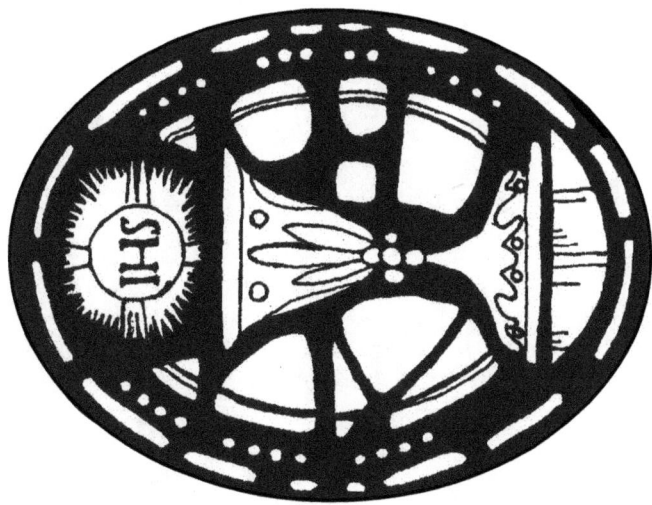

Luminary Bottom
Cut and remove this
circle for light.

© copyright 2016 Corinne M. Shibley. HGBG Productions. All rights reserved.

CAUTION: these luminaries are not to be used with an open flame or heat producing bulbs.

www.coloringlight.com

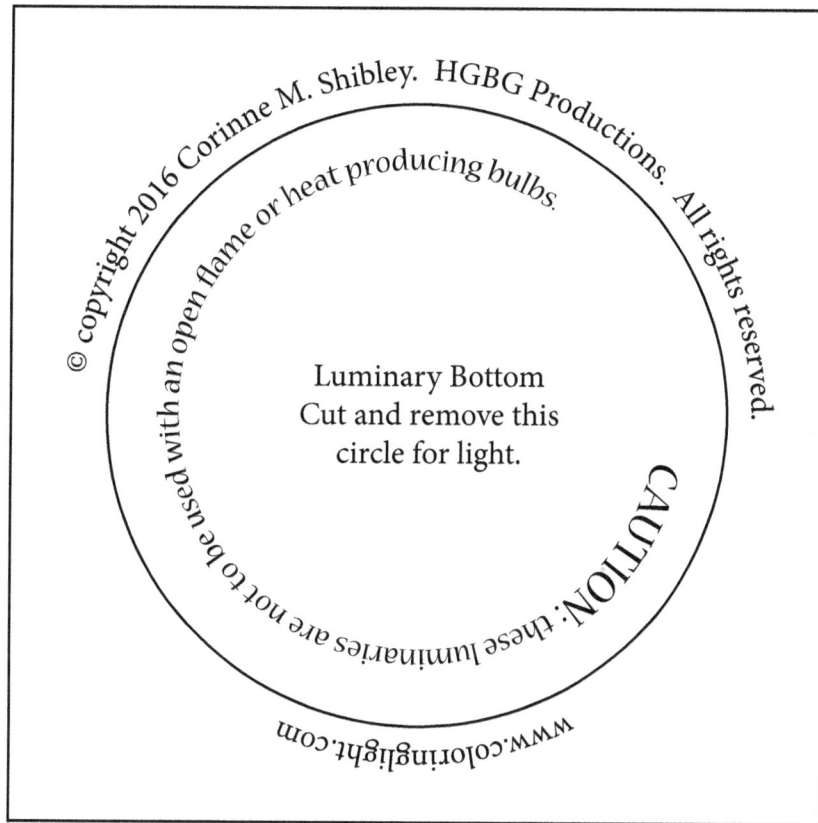

Luminary Top, cut just inside of lines

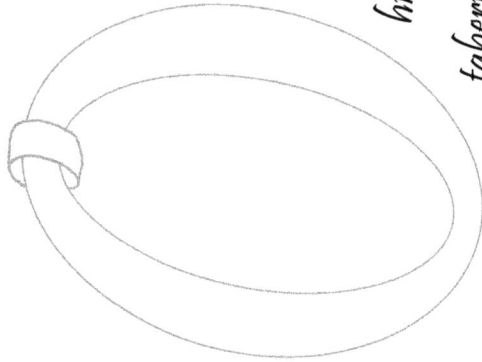

h, send out Your light
and Your truth! Let
them lead me; let them
bring me to Your holy
hill And to Your
tabernacle.   Psalm 43:3

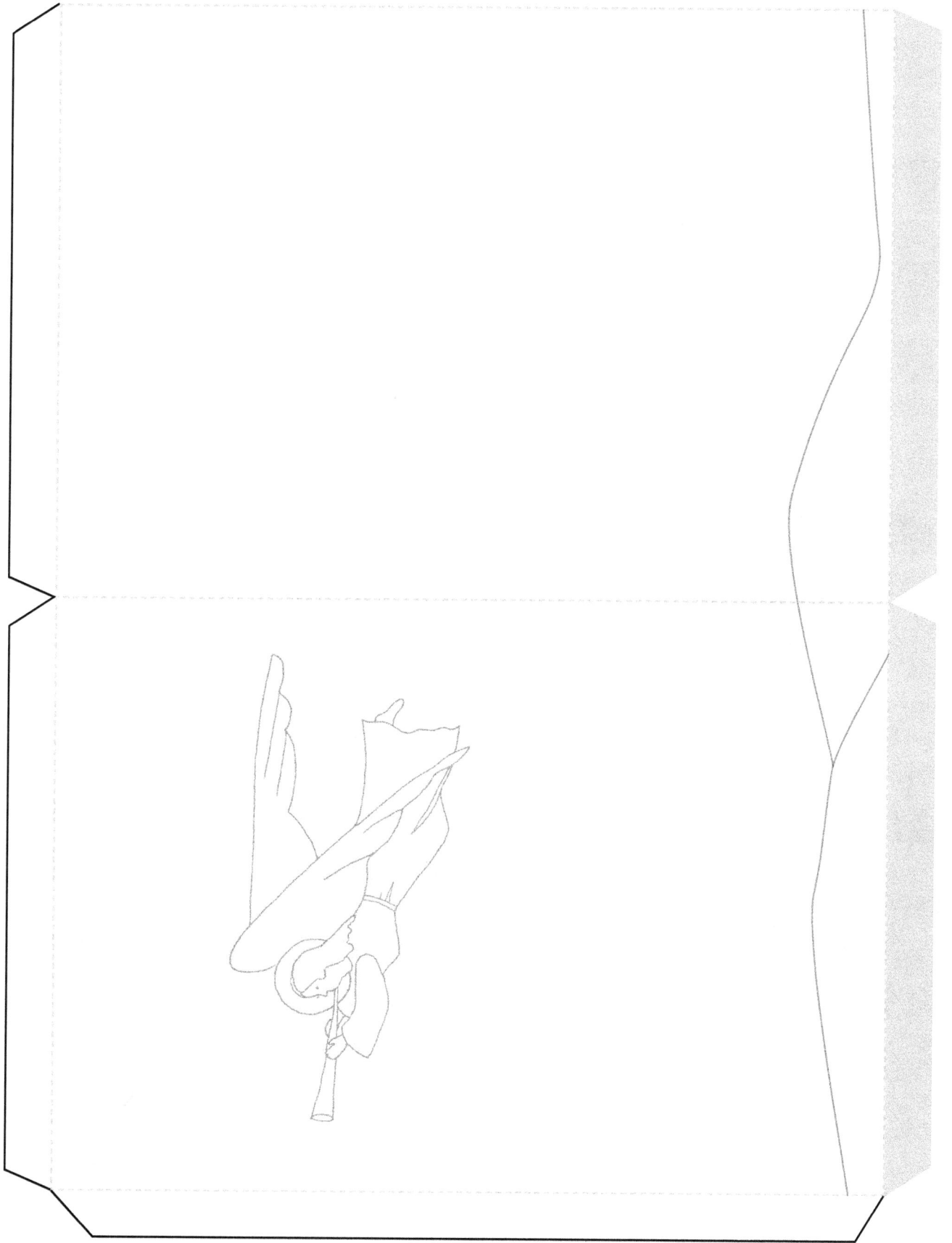

© copyright 2016 Corinne M. Shibley. HGBG Productions. All rights reserved.

CAUTION: these luminaries are not to be used with an open flame or heat producing bulbs.

www.coloringlight.com

Luminary Bottom
Cut and remove this
circle for light.

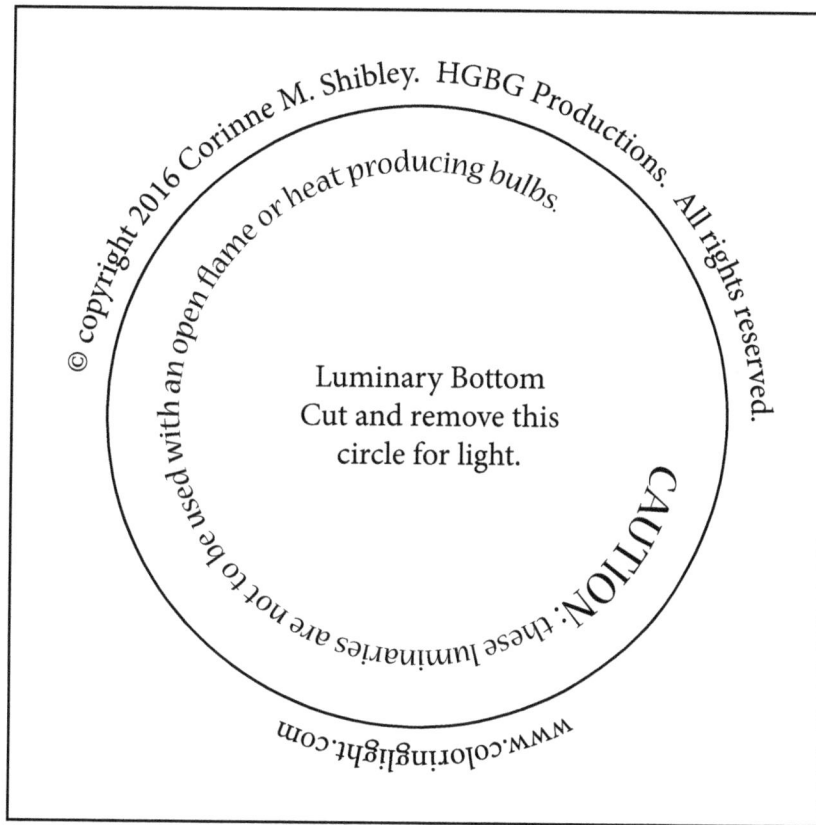

Luminary Top, cut just inside of lines

the truth, and the life.

esus said to him,
"I am the way,

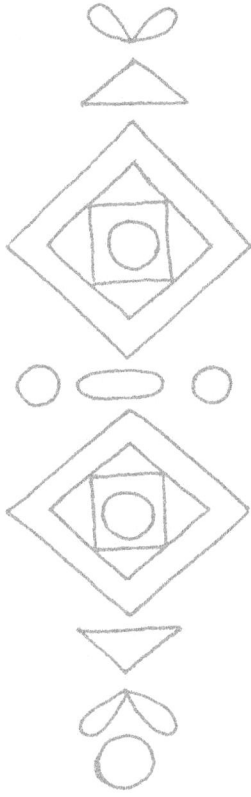

except through Me"

John 14:6

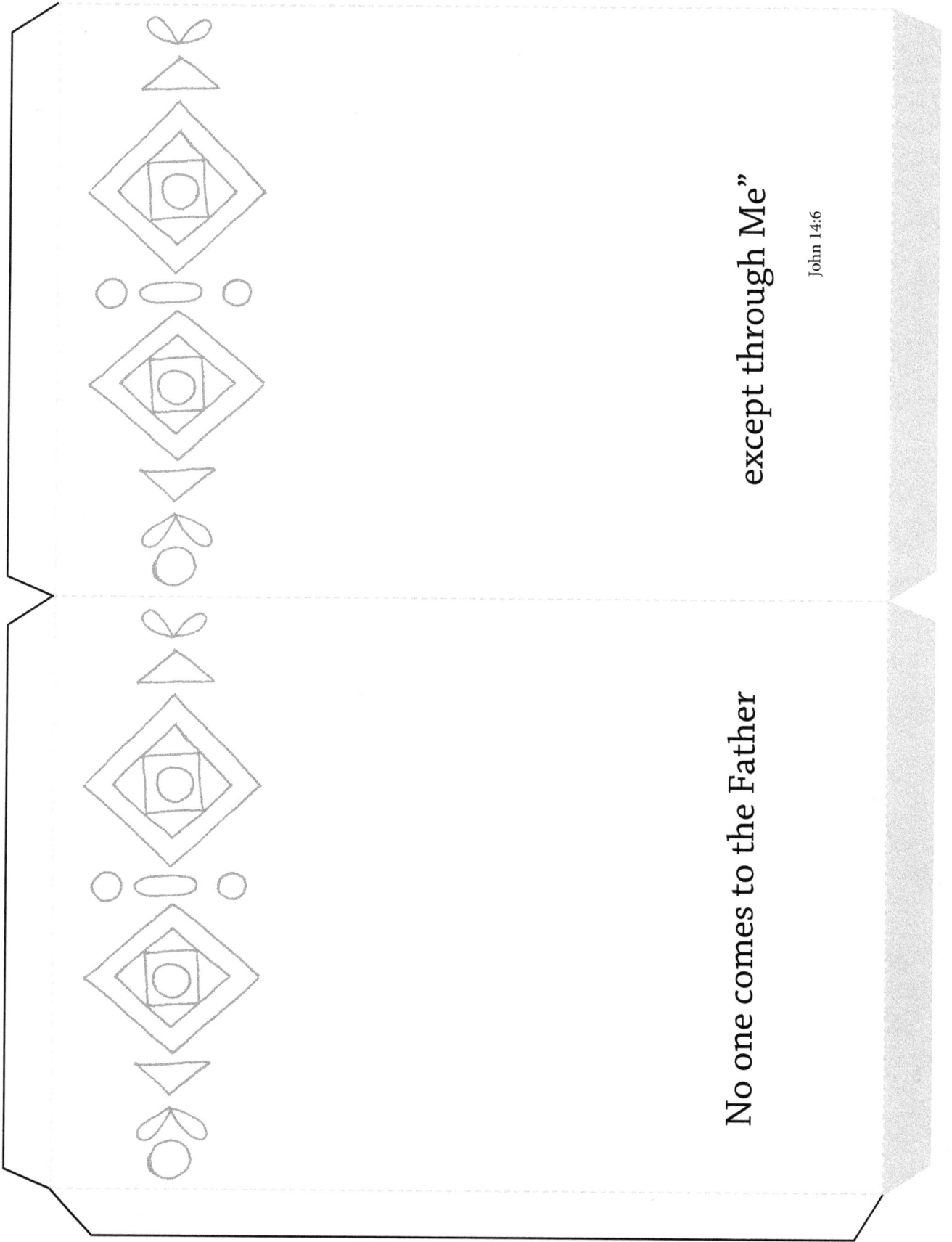

No one comes to the Father

Luminary Bottom
Cut and remove this
circle for light.

© copyright 2016 Corinne M. Shibley. HGBG Productions. All rights reserved.

CAUTION: these luminaries are not to be used with an open flame or heat producing bulbs.

www.coloringlight.com

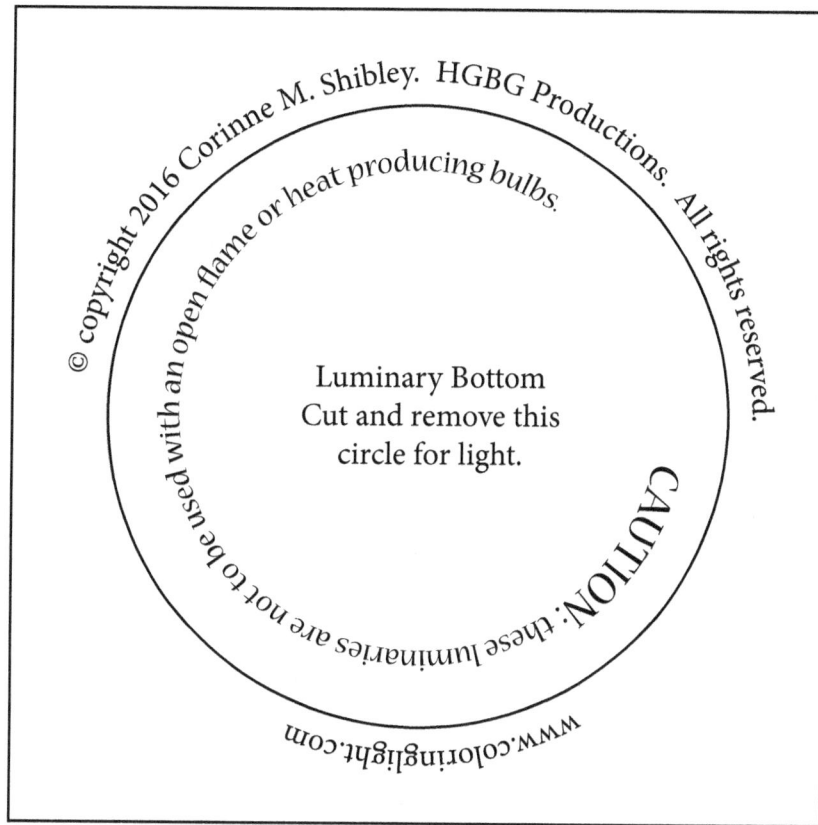

Luminary Top, cut just inside of lines

I am the light of the world. He who follows Me shall not walk in darkness, but have the light of life.

John 8:12

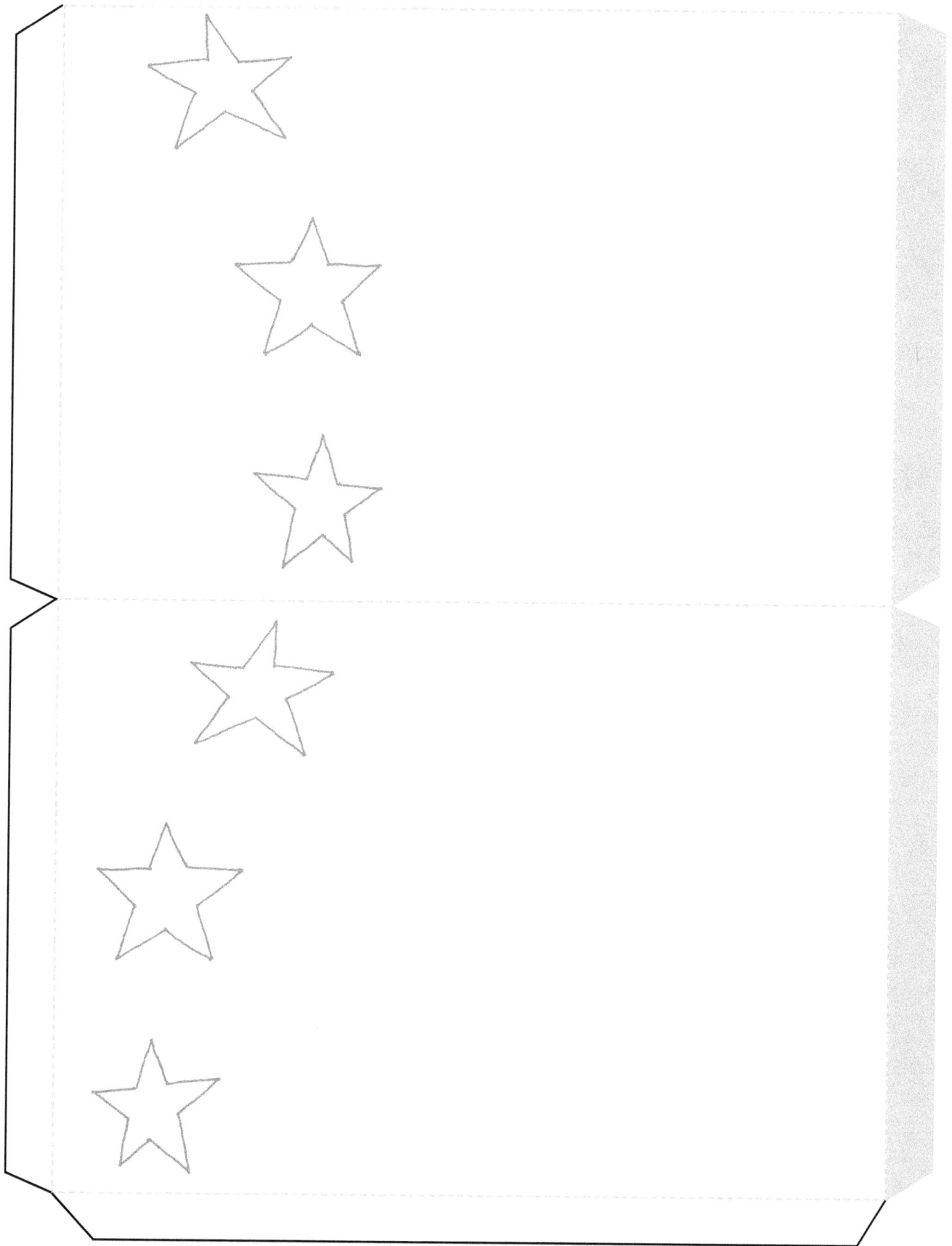

Luminary Bottom
Cut and remove this
circle for light.

© copyright 2016 Corinne M. Shibley. HGBG Productions. All rights reserved.

CAUTION: these luminaries are not to be used with an open flame or heat producing bulbs.

www.coloringlight.com

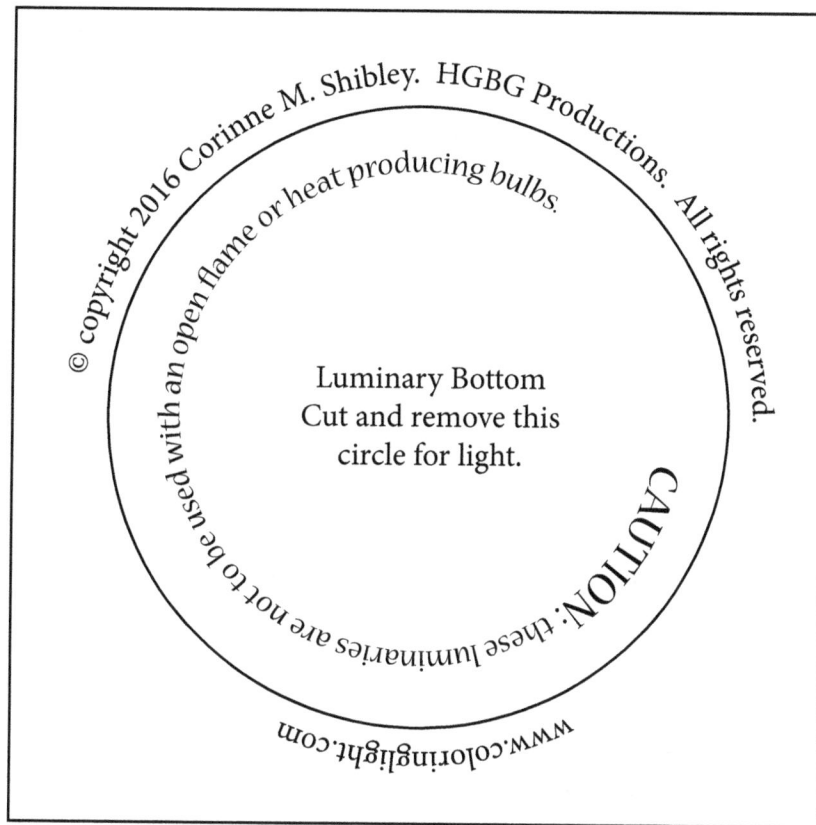

Luminary Top, cut just inside of lines

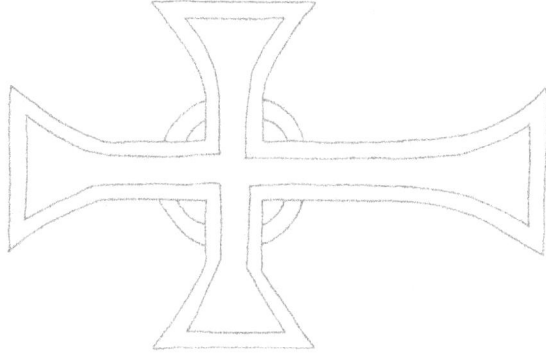

I

am the Lord, and there is no other; I form the light and create darkness, I make peace and create calamity; I the Lord, do all these things.

Isaiah 45:6-7

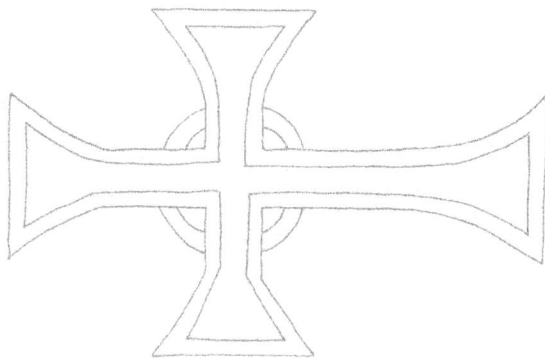

Luminary Bottom
Cut and remove this
circle for light.

© copyright 2016 Corinne M. Shibley. HGBG Productions. All rights reserved.

CAUTION: these luminaries are not to be used with an open flame or heat producing bulbs.

www.coloringlight.com

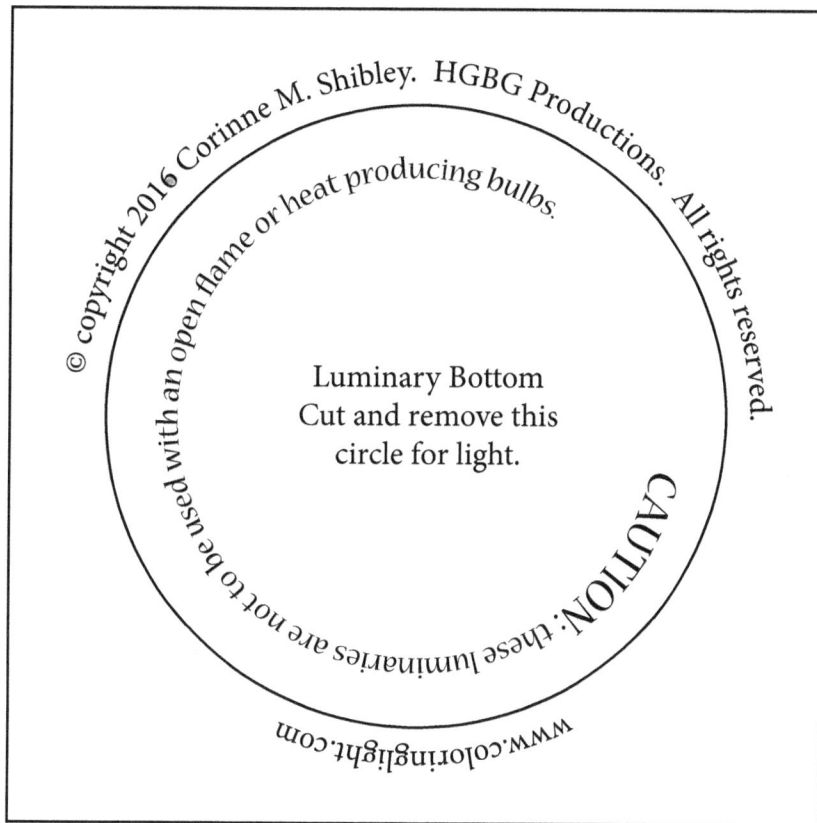

Luminary Top, cut just inside of lines

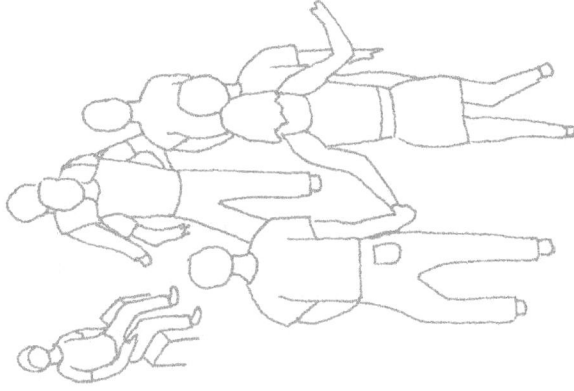

for wide is the gate and broad is

nter by the narrow gate;

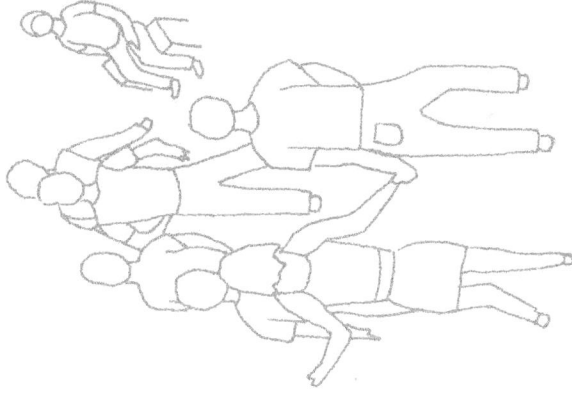

and there are many who go in by it.

Matthew 7:13

the way that leads to destruction,

© copyright 2016 Corinne M. Shibley. HGBG Productions. All rights reserved

CAUTION: these luminaries are not to be used with an open flame or heat producing bulbs.

www.coloringlight.com.

Luminary Bottom
Cut and remove this
circle for light.

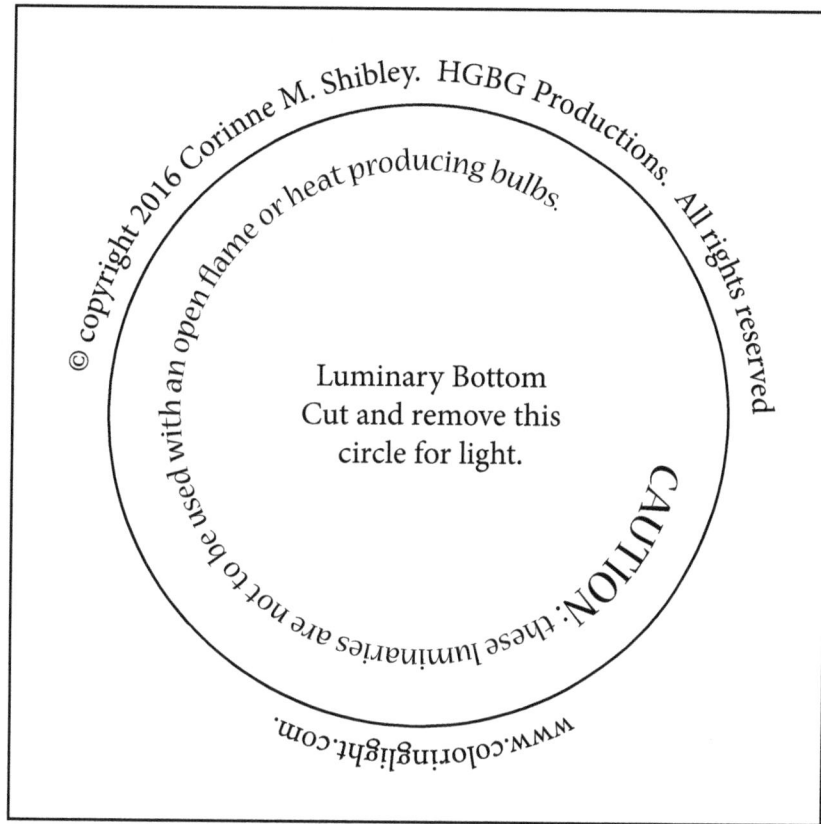

Luminary Top, cut just inside of lines

He was in the beginning with God.

n the beginning was the Word, and the Word was with God, and the Word was God.

In Him was life, and the life was the light of men.   John 1:1-4

All things were made through Him, and without Him nothing was made that was made.

© copyright 2016 Corinne M. Shibley. HGBG Productions. All rights reserved.

CAUTION: these luminaries are not to be used with an open flame or heat producing bulbs.

www.coloringlight.com

Luminary Bottom
Cut and remove this
circle for light.

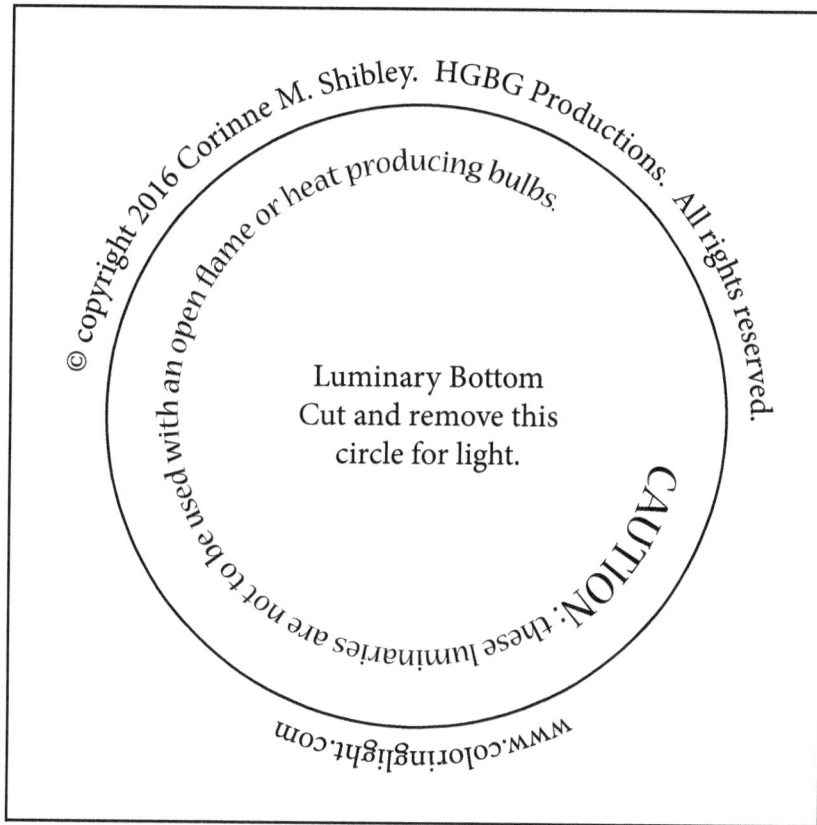

Luminary Top, cut just inside of lines

ou are
the light
of the world.
A city that
is set on a hill
cannot be hid-
den. Nor do they
light a lamp and put
it under a basket, but
on a lampstand, and it
gives light to all who
are in the house. Let
your light so shine
before men, that they
may see your good works and
glorify your Father in heaven.

Matthew 5:14-16

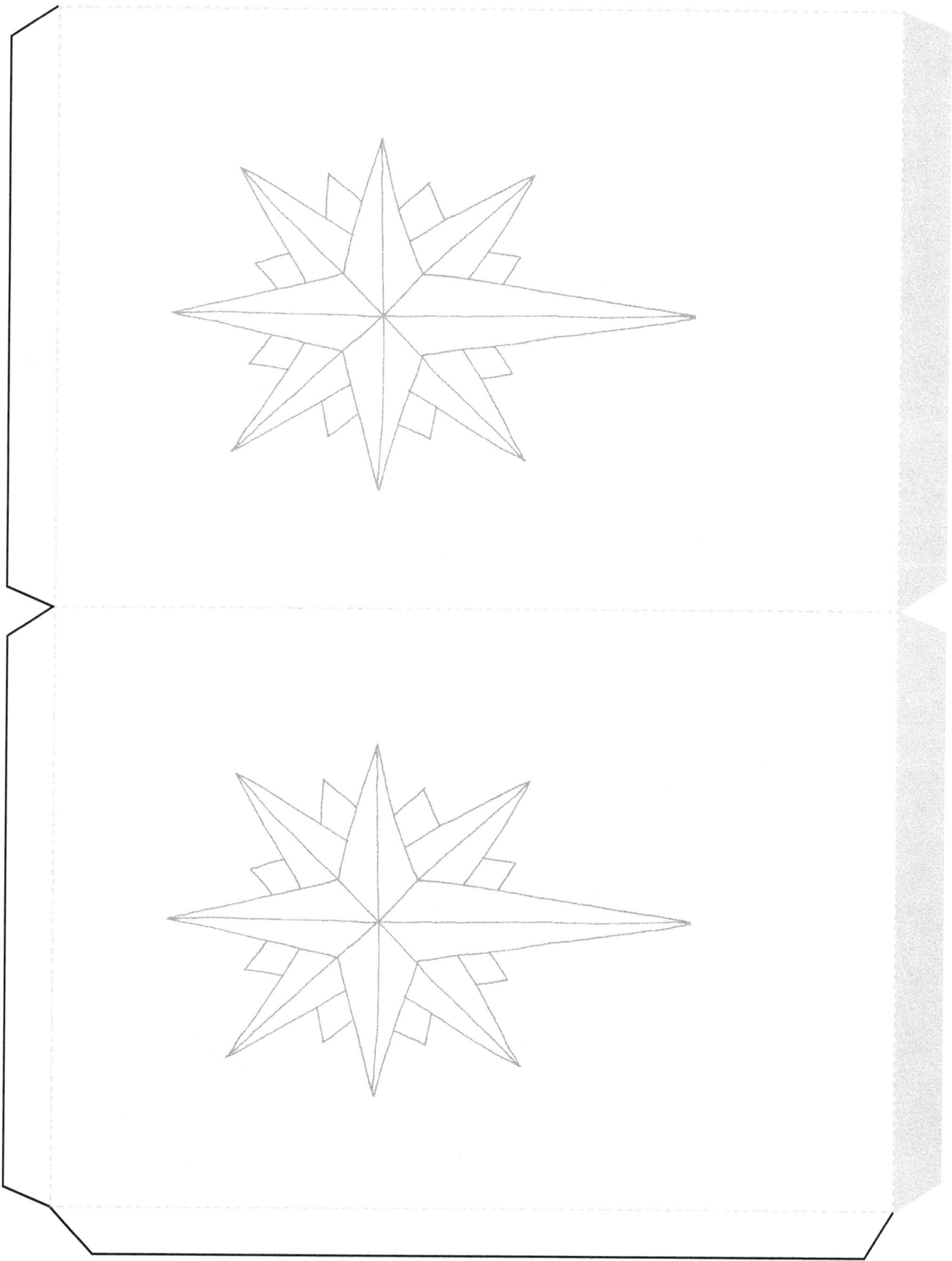

© copyright 2016 Corinne M. Shibley. HGBG Productions. All rights reserved.

CAUTION: these luminaries are not to be used with an open flame or heat producing bulbs.

www.coloringlight.com

Luminary Bottom
Cut and remove this
circle for light.

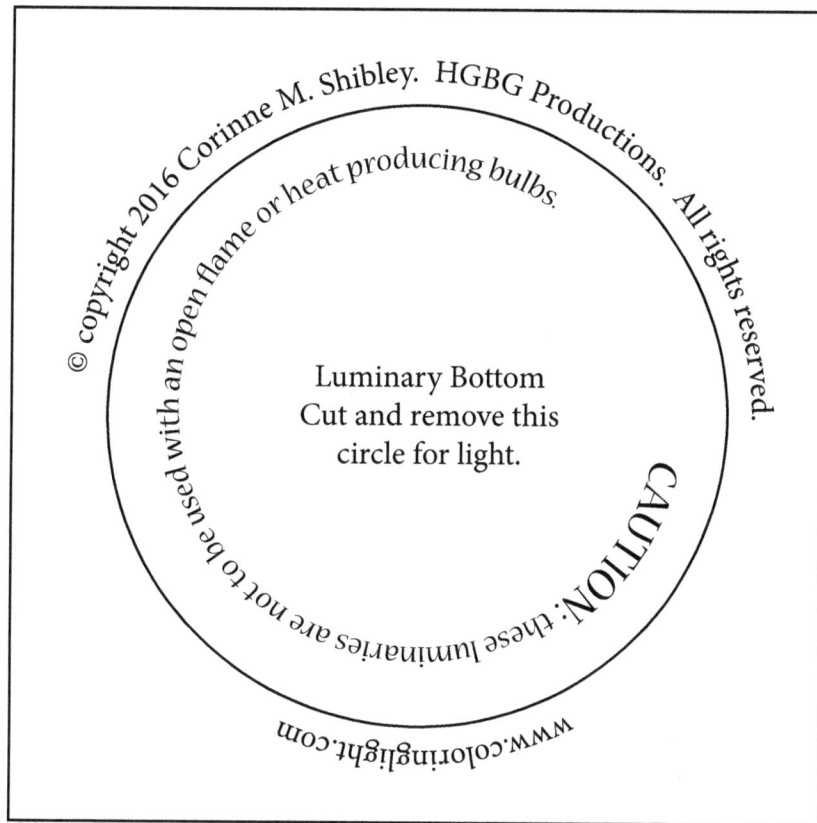

Luminary Top, cut just inside of lines

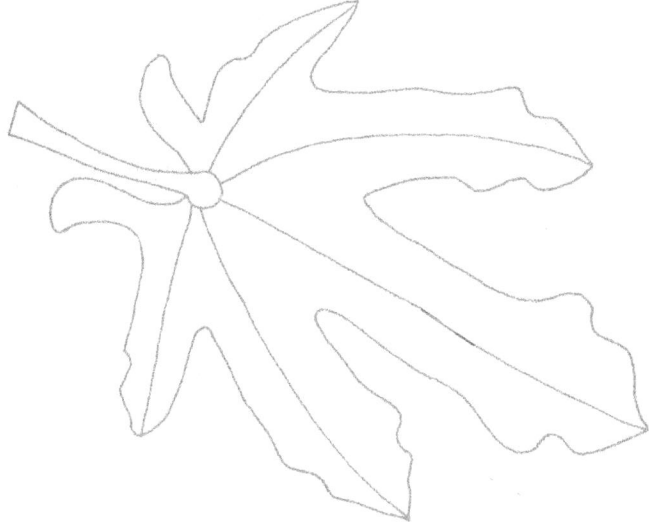

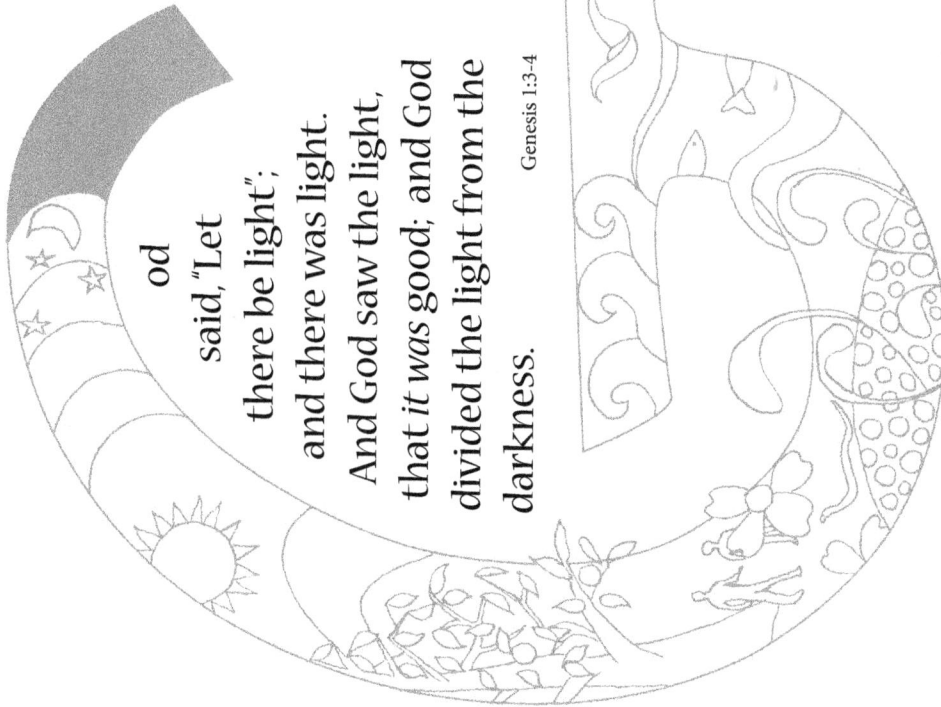

od said, "Let there be light"; and there was light. And God saw the light, that *it was* good; and God divided the light from the darkness.

Genesis 1:3-4

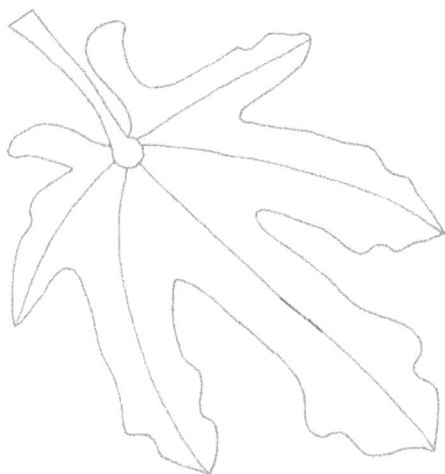

© copyright 2016 Corinne M. Shibley. HGBG Productions. All rights reserved.

CAUTION: these luminaries are not to be used with an open flame or heat producing bulbs.

www.coloringlight.com

Luminary Bottom
Cut and remove this
circle for light.

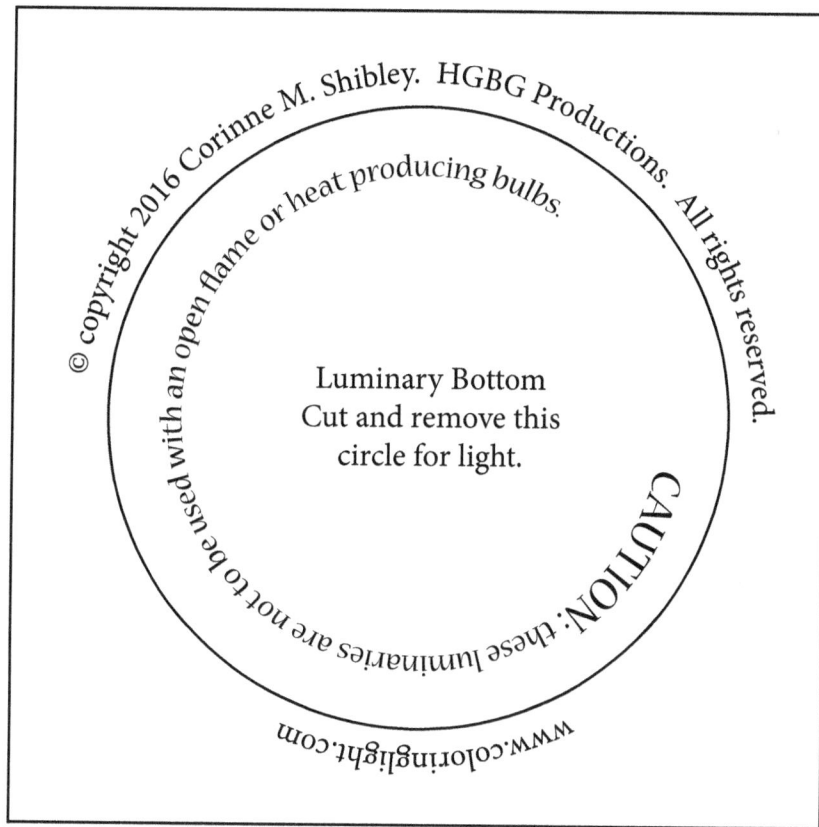

Luminary Top, cut just inside of lines

and walks in darkness,

ut

he who hates his brother is in darkness

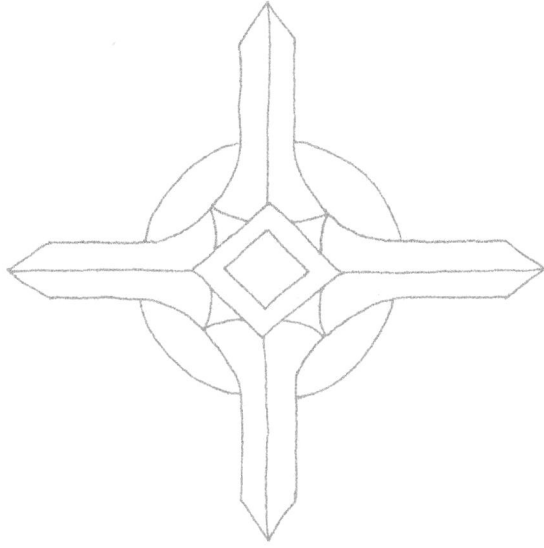

because the darkness has blinded his eyes.

1 John:2:11

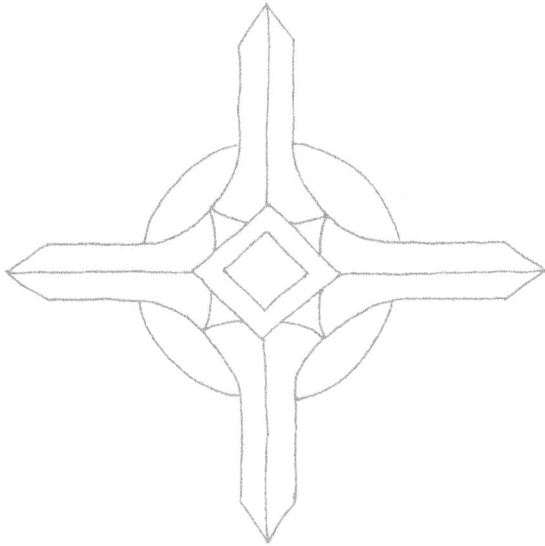

and does not know where he is going,

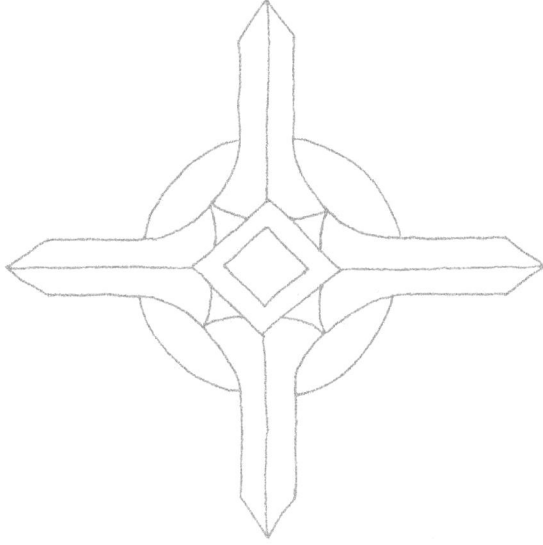

© copyright 2016 Corinne M. Shibley. HGBG Productions. All rights reserved.

CAUTION: these luminaries are not to be used with an open flame or heat producing bulbs.

www.coloringlight.com

Luminary Bottom
Cut and remove this
circle for light.

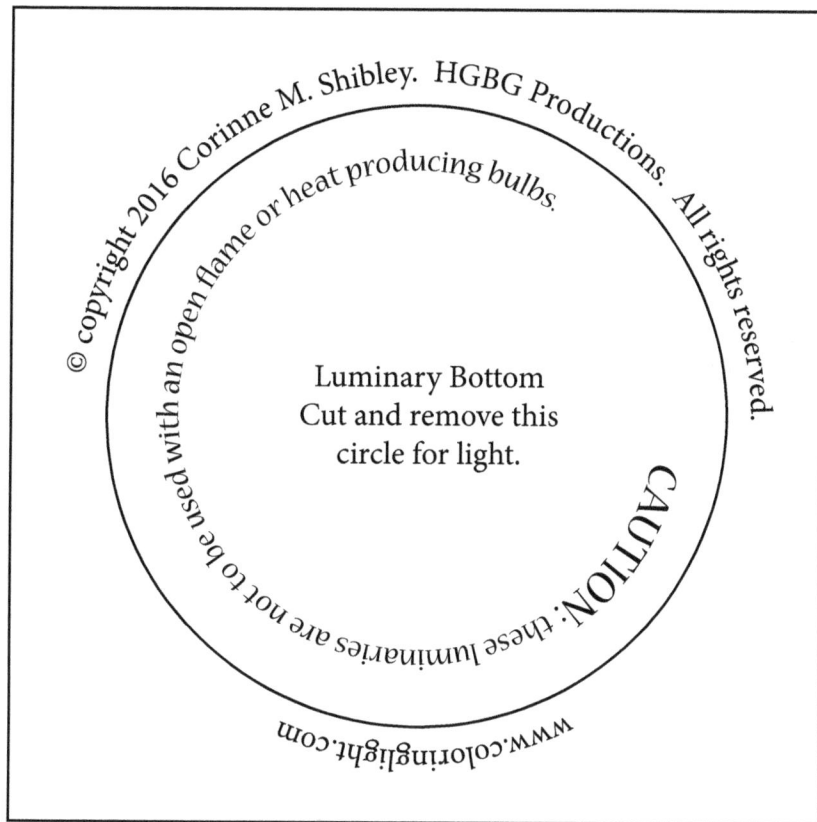

Luminary Top, cut just inside of lines

and my salvation;

he LORD
is my
light

Whom shall I fear?

Psalm 27:1

Luminary Bottom
Cut and remove this
circle for light.

© copyright 2016 Corinne M. Shibley. HGBG Productions. All rights reserved.

CAUTION: these luminaries are not to be used with an open flame or heat producing bulbs.

www.coloringlight.com

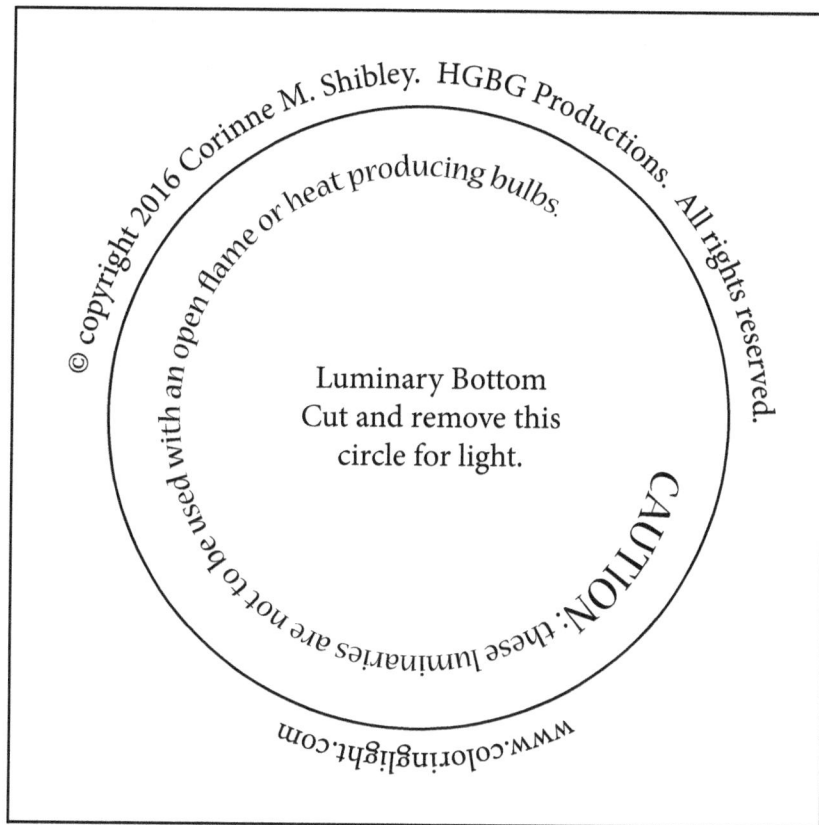

Luminary Top, cut just inside of lines

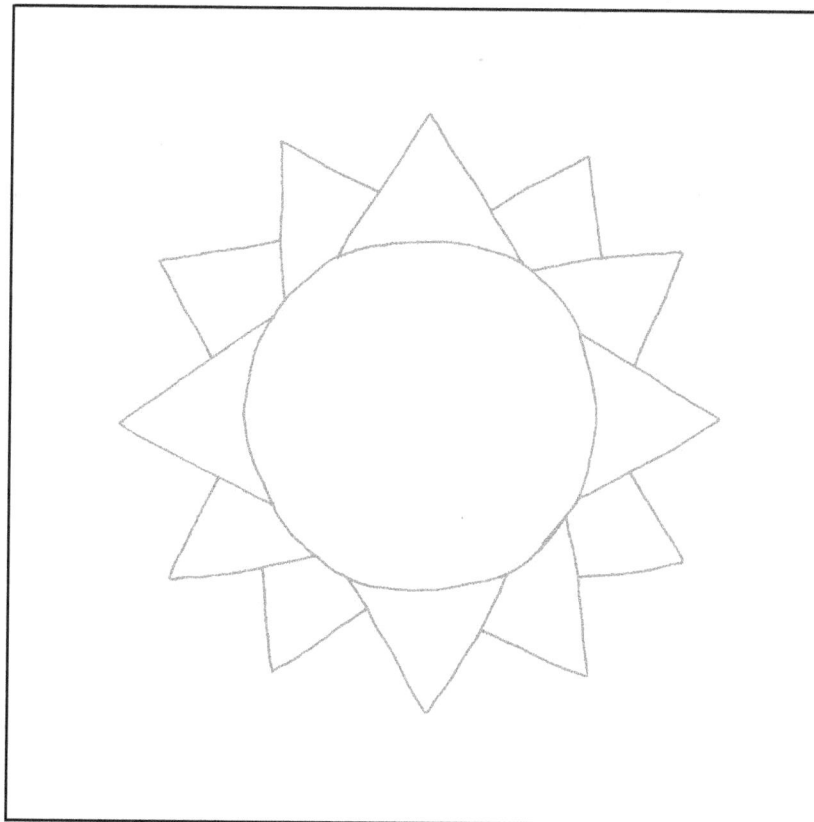

THE HAND OF THE LORD
CAME UPON ME AND
BROUGHT ME OUT IN THE
SPIRIT OF THE LORD,

AND SET ME
DOWN IN
THE MIDST
OF THE VAL
LEY, AND IT
WAS FULL OF
BONES

BONES CAME TOGETHER,
A RATTLING, AND THE
NOISE, AND SUDDENLY
THERE WAS A
AS I PROPHESIED,

Ezekiel 37:1

BONE
TO
BONE
INDEED, AS
I LOOKED,
AND THE
SINEWS
AND THE FLESH
CAME UPON
THEM, AND THE
SKIN COVERED
OVER, BUT THERE
WAS NO BREATH IN
THEM, BUT THERE
BREATH IN
THEM.

Ezekiel 37:7-8

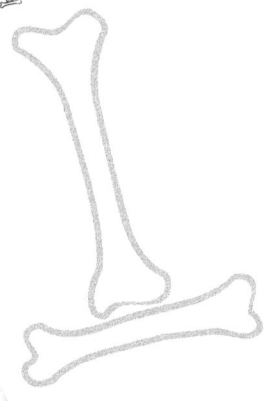

THUS SAYS
THE LORD
GOD: "COME
FROM THE FOUR
WINDS, O BREATH,
AND BREATHE ON
THESE SLAIN, THAT
THEY MAY LIVE."

SO I
PROPHESIED
AS HE
COMMANDED ME,
AND BREATH CAME
INTO THEM, AND
THEY LIVED,

AND STOOD
UPON THEIR
FEET, AN EX
CEEDINGLY GREAT
ARMY.

Ezekiel 37:9-10

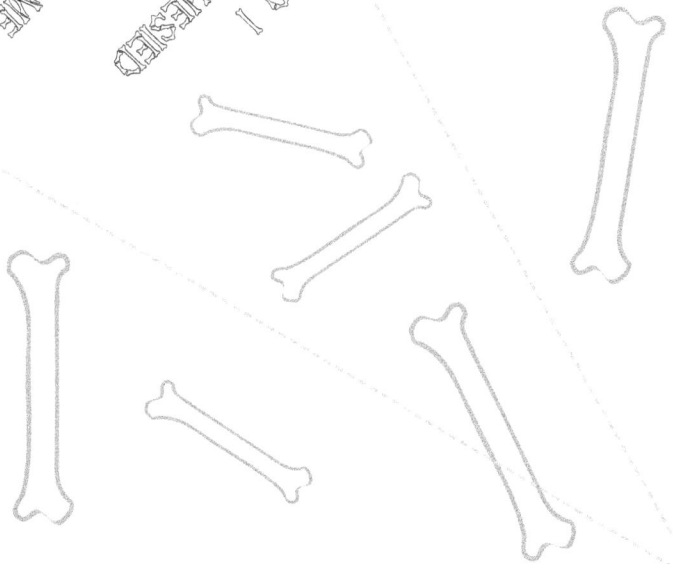

Luminary Bottom
Cut and remove this
circle for light.

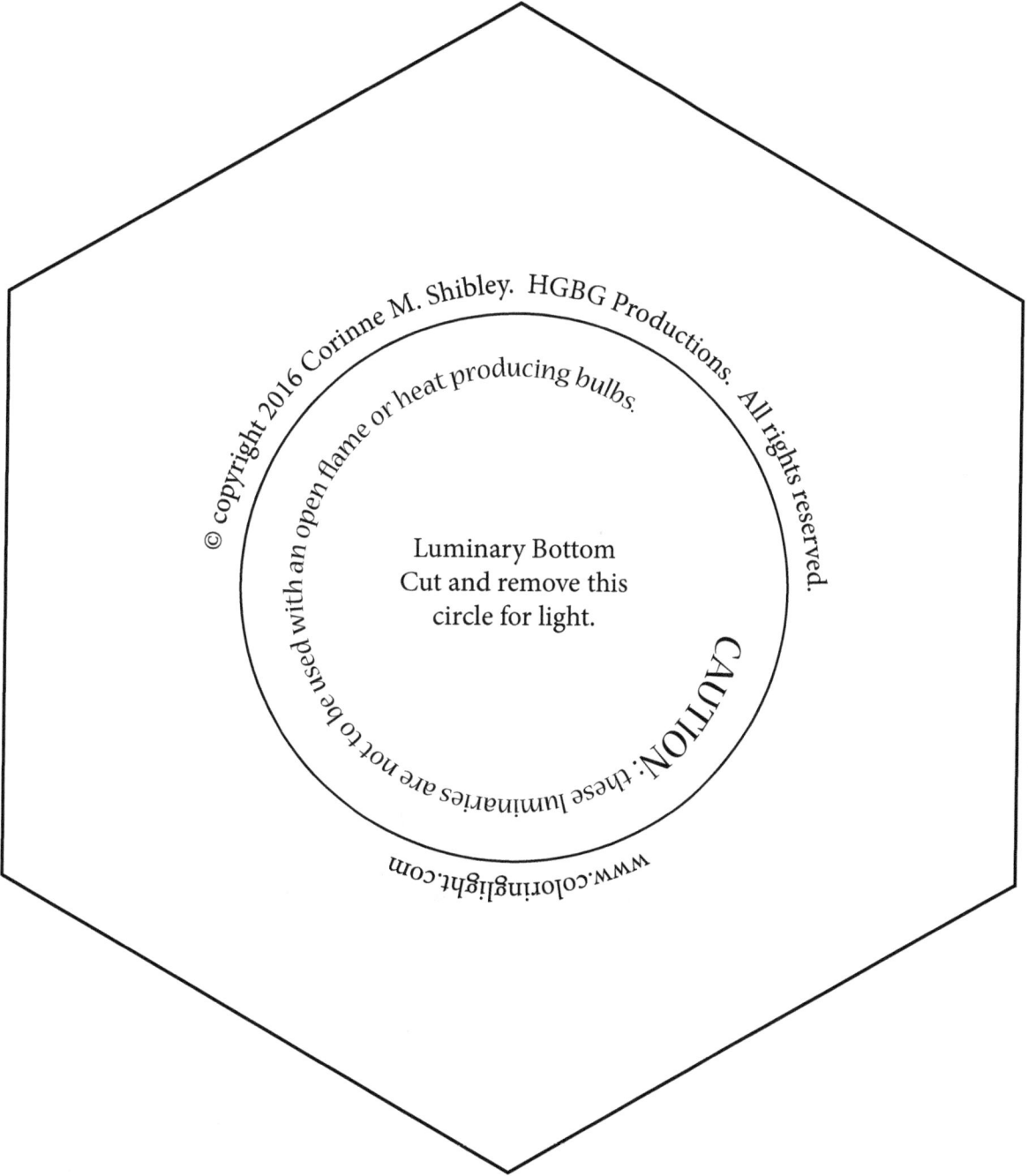

© copyright 2016 Corinne M. Shibley. HGBG Productions. All rights reserved.

CAUTION: these luminaries are not to be used with an open flame or heat producing bulbs.

www.coloringlight.com

you are My disciples indeed.

f you abide in My word,

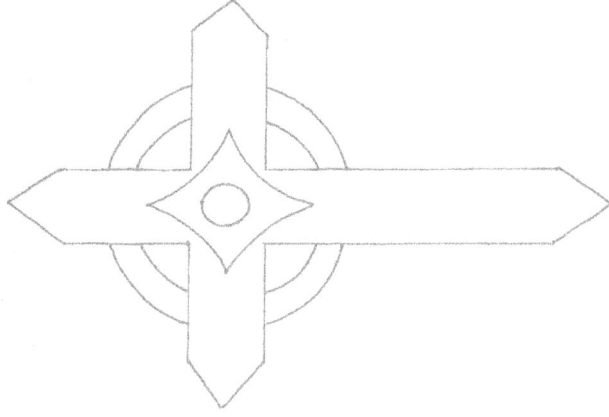

and the truth shall make you free."

John 8:31-32

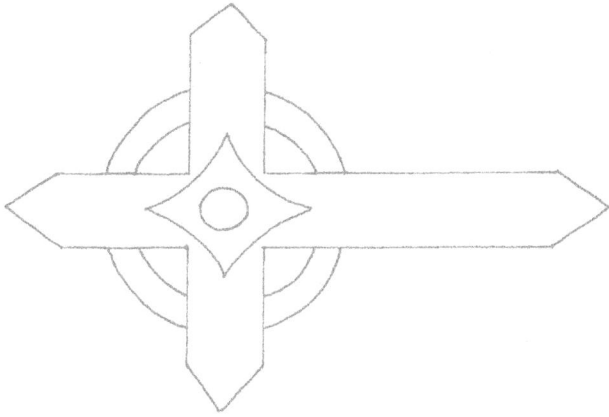

And you shall know the truth,

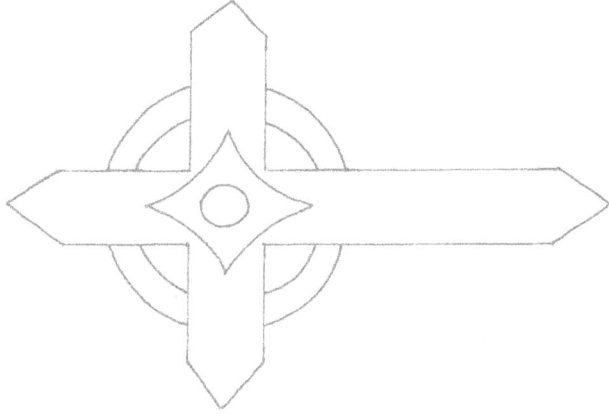

© copyright 2016 Corinne M. Shibley. HGBG Productions. All rights reserved

Luminary Bottom
Cut and remove this
circle for light.

CAUTION: these luminaries are not to be used with an open flame or heat producing bulbs.

www.coloringlight.com.

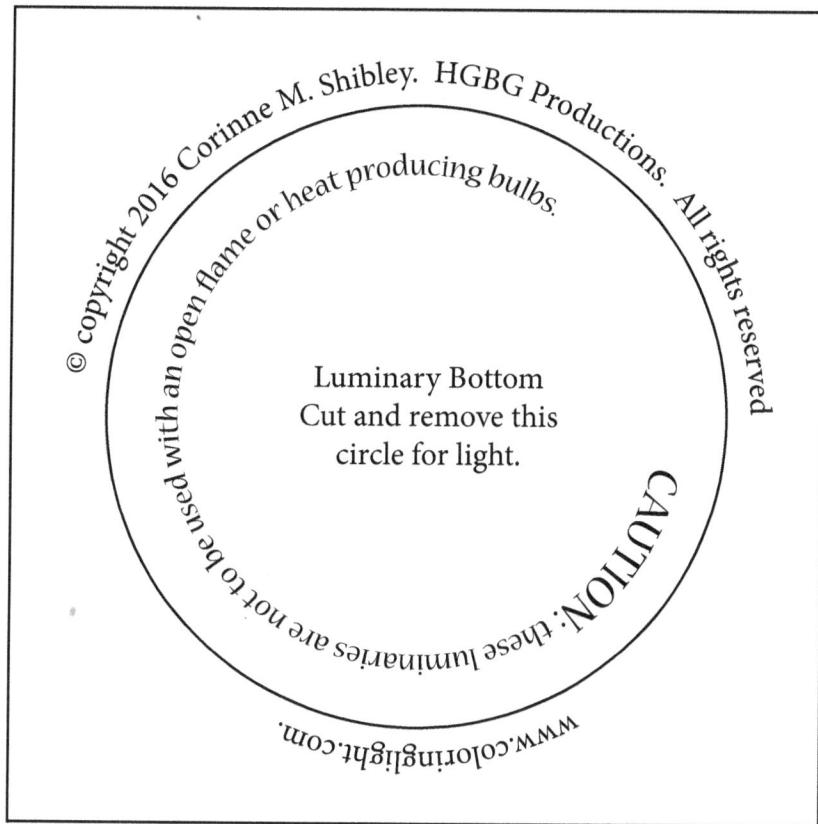

Luminary Top, cut just inside of lines

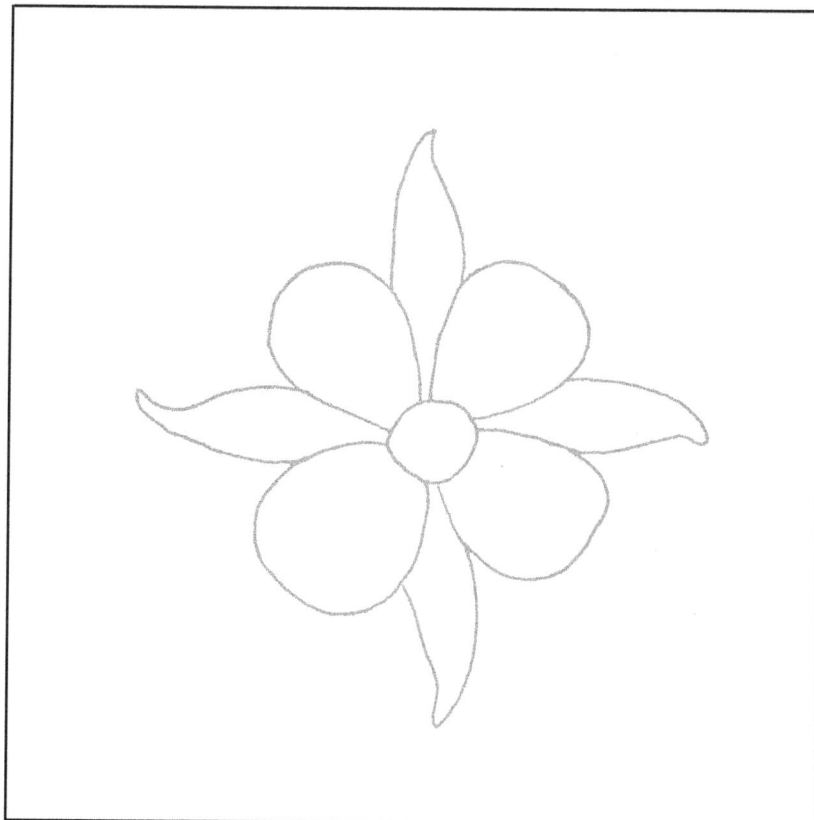

give to him glorious praise!

hout for joy to God, all the earth;
sing the glory of his name;

Come and see what God has done:

he is awesome in his deeds toward the
children of man.   Psalm 66:1-2,5 ESV

Luminary Bottom
Cut and remove this
circle for light.

© copyright 2016 Corinne M. Shibley. HGBG Productions. All rights reserved.

CAUTION: these luminaries are not to be used with an open flame or heat producing bulbs.

www.coloringlight.com

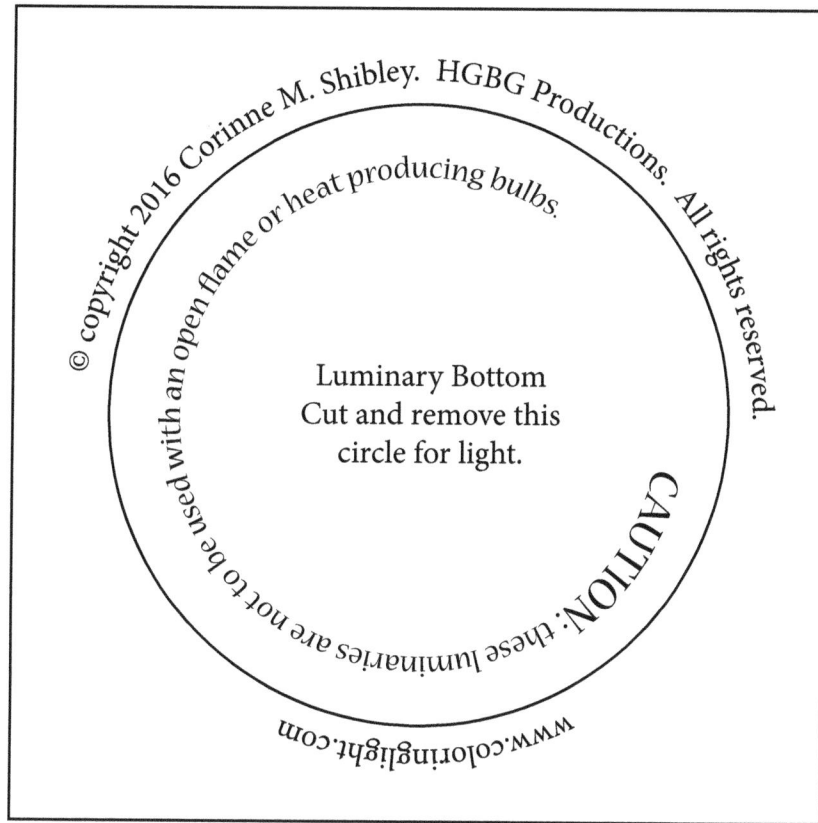

Luminary Top, cut just inside of lines

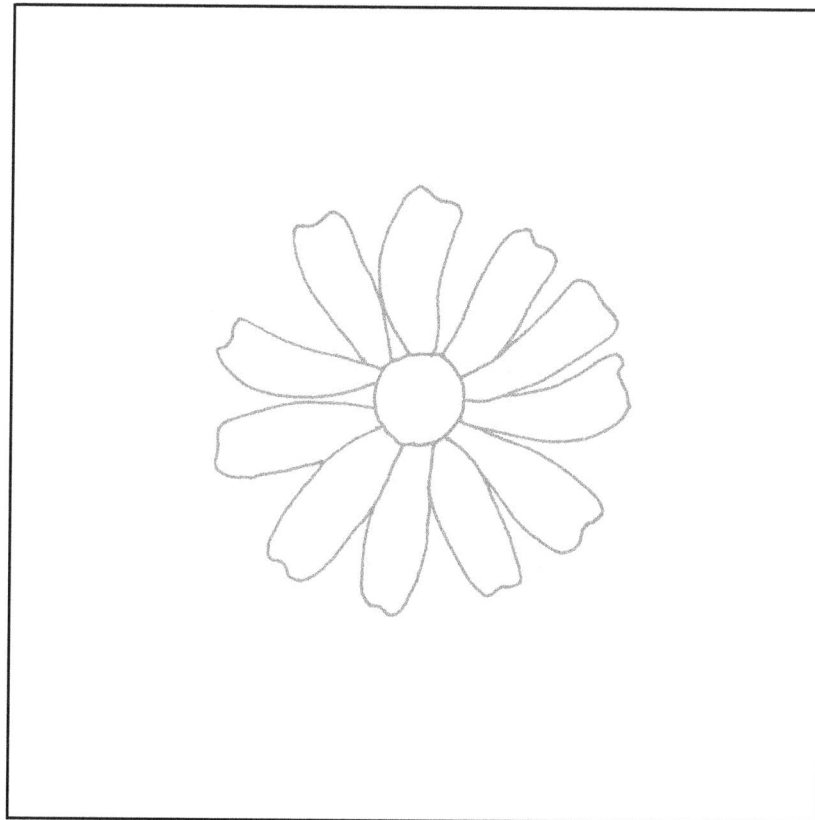

VI

Thou shalt not kill

VII

Thou shalt not commit adultery

VIII

Thou shalt not steal

IX

Thou shalt not bear false witness against thy neighbour

X

Thou shalt not covet

Exodus 20 KJV

I

Thou shalt have no other gods before me

II

Thou shalt not make unto thee any graven image

III

Thou shalt not take the name of the LORD thy God in vain

IV

Remember the sabbath day, to keep it holy

V

Honour thy father and thy mother

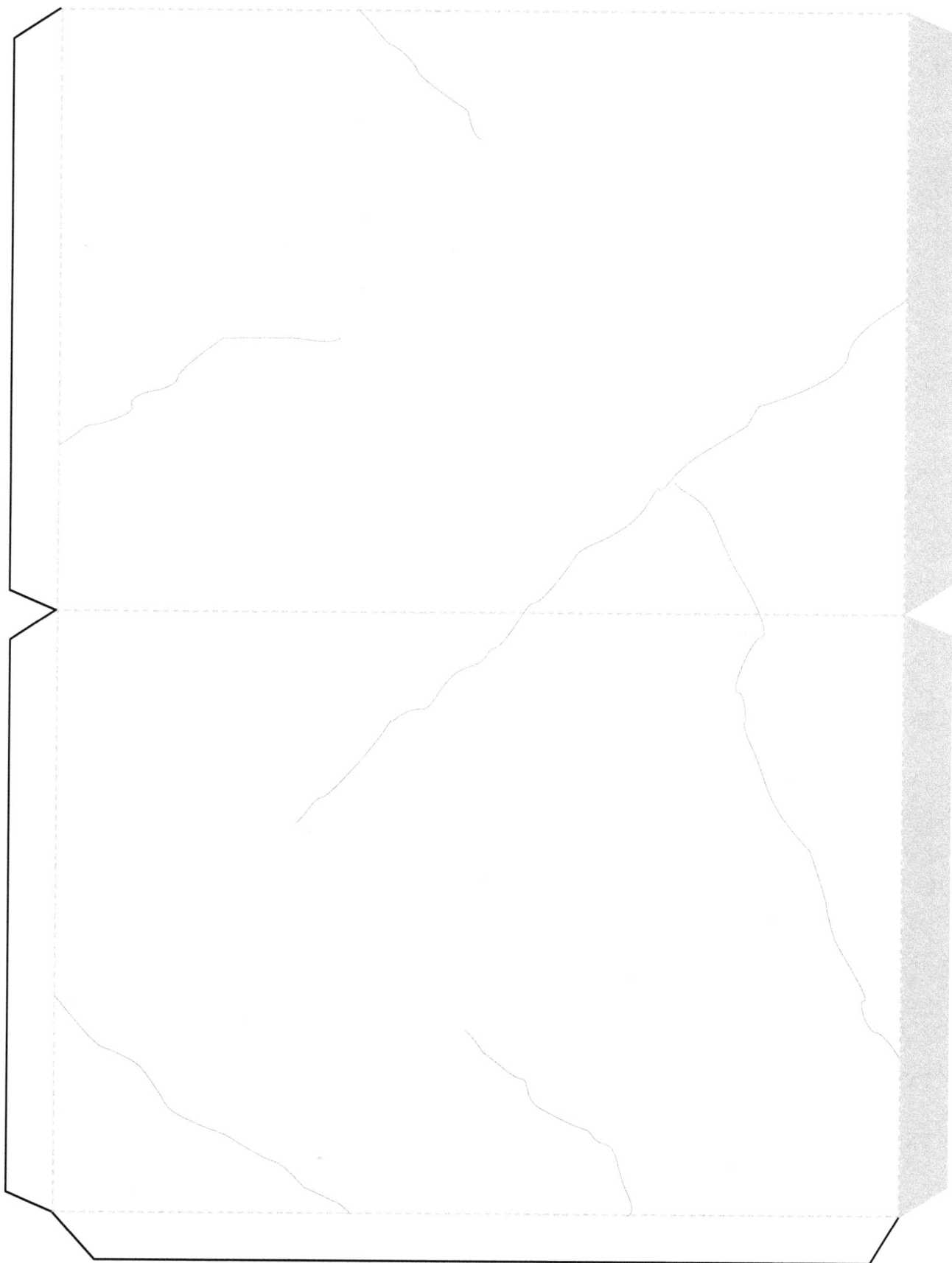

Luminary Bottom
Cut and remove this
circle for light.

© copyright 2016 Corinne M. Shibley. HGBG Productions. All rights reserved.

CAUTION: these luminaries are not to be used with an open flame or heat producing bulbs.

www.coloringlight.com

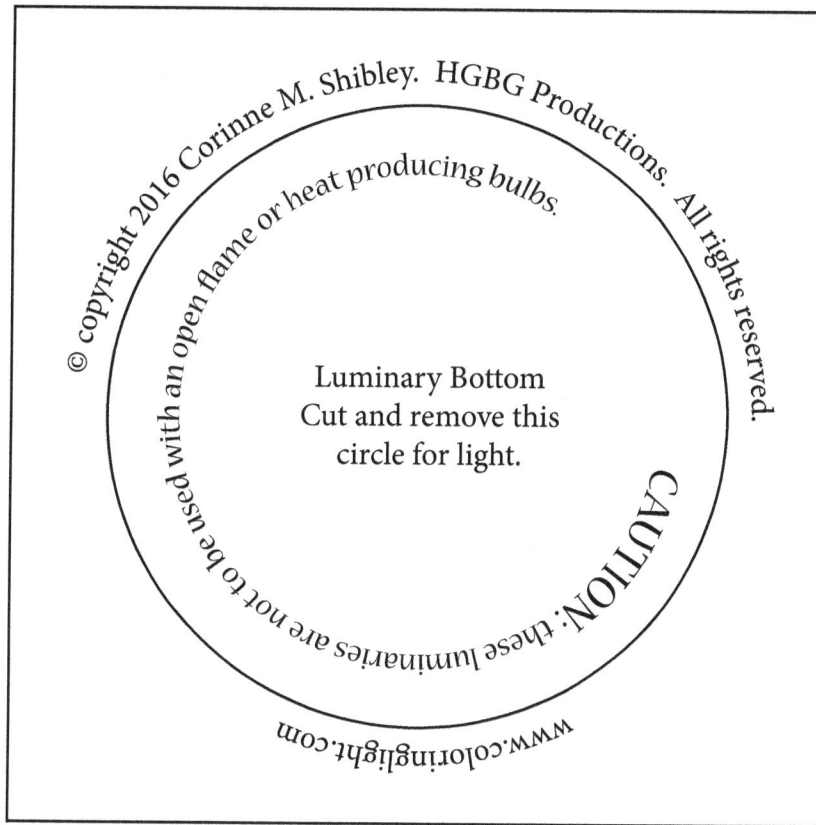

Luminary Top, cut just inside of lines

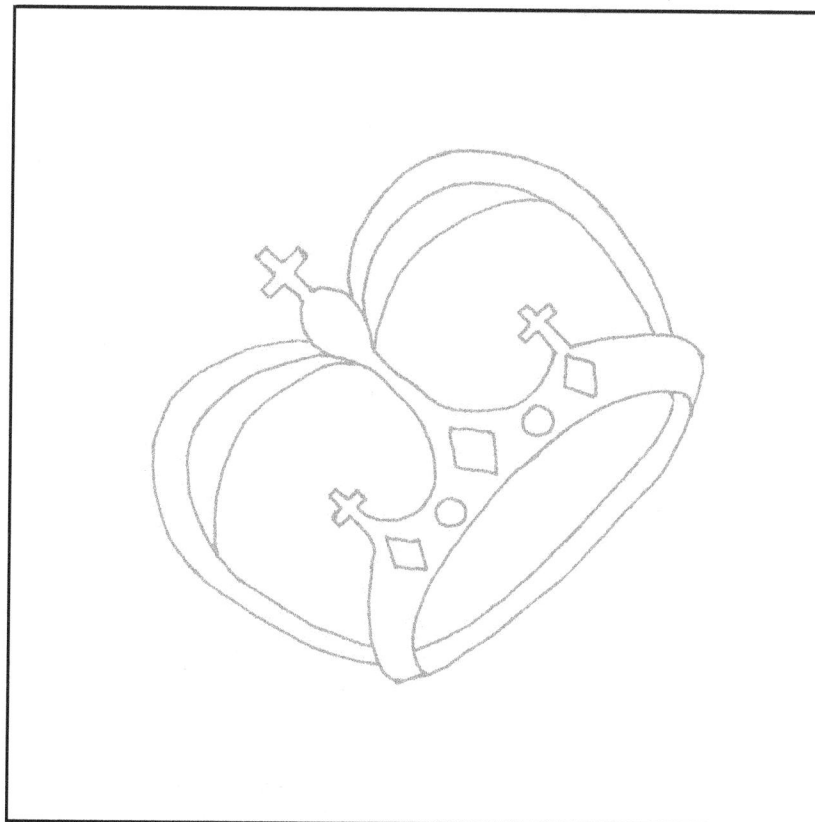

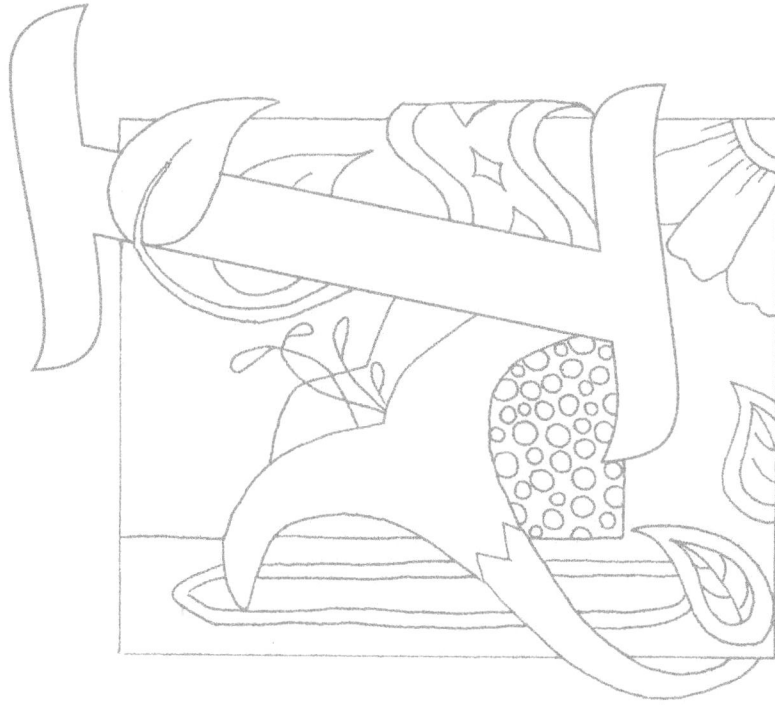

the Lord, have called You in righteousness,

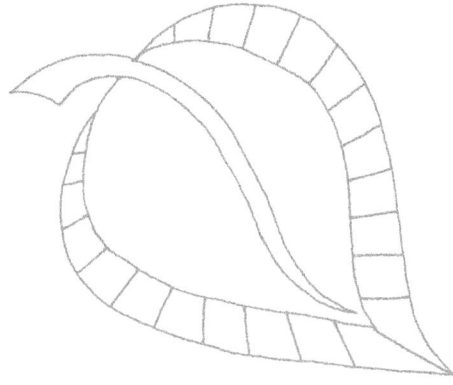

And will hold Your hand;

As a light to the gentiles...

Isaiah 42:6

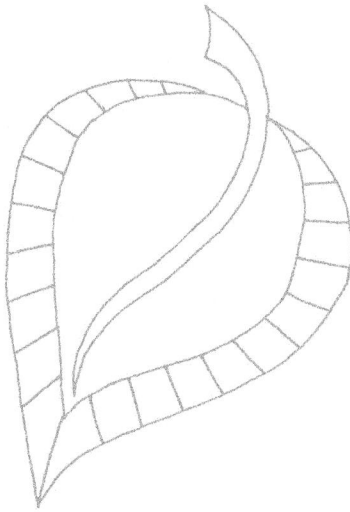

I will keep You and give you as a covenant to the people,

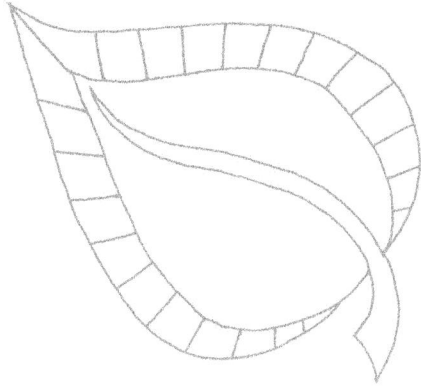

© copyright 2016 Corinne M. Shibley. HGBG Productions. All rights reserved.

CAUTION: these luminaries are not to be used with an open flame or heat producing bulbs.

www.coloringlight.com

Luminary Bottom
Cut and remove this
circle for light.

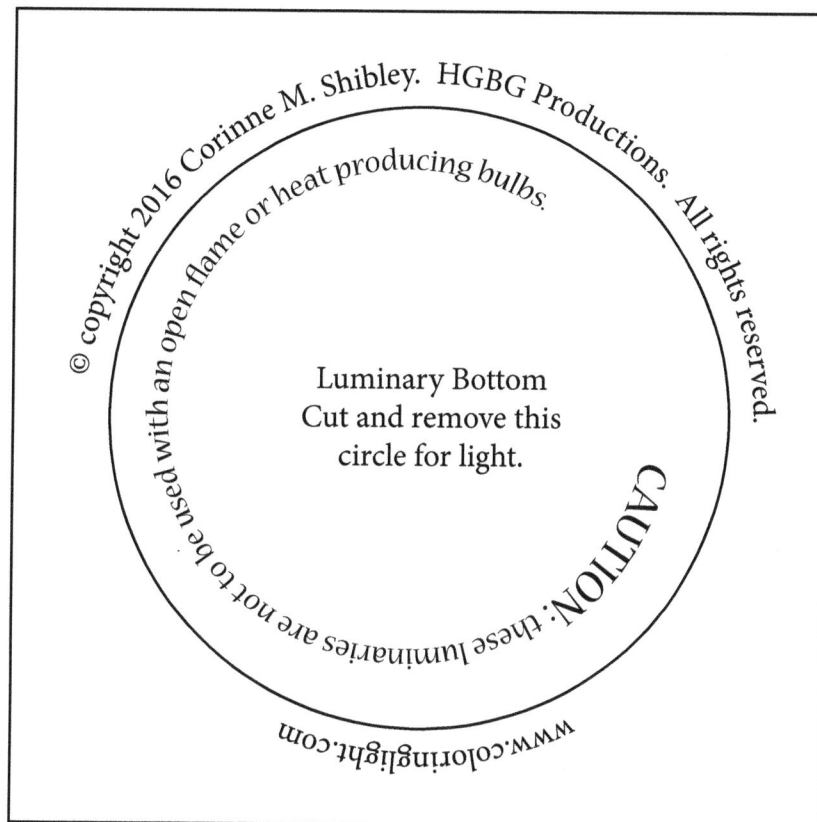

Luminary Top, cut just inside of lines

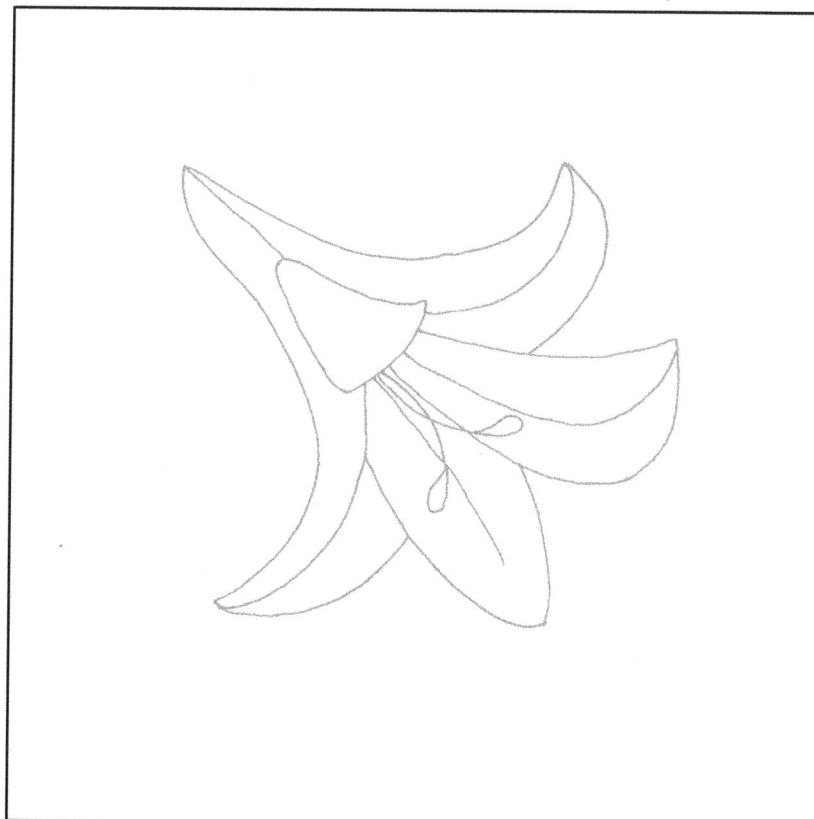

My soul thirsts for You;
My flesh longs for You

God, You are my God;
Early will I seek You;

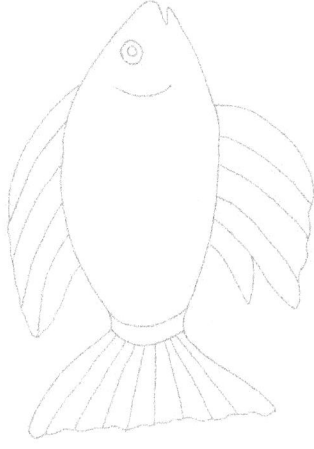

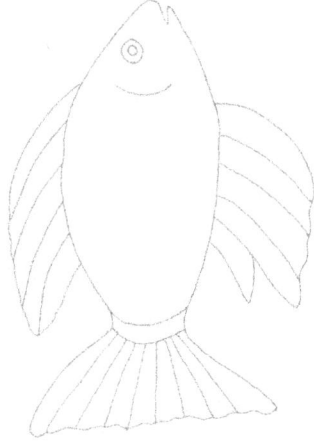

Where there is no water.   Psalm 63:1

In a dry and thirsty land

Luminary Bottom
Cut and remove this
circle for light.

© copyright 2016 Corinne M. Shibley. HGBG Productions. All rights reserved.

CAUTION: these luminaries are not to be used with an open flame or heat producing bulbs.

www.coloringlight.com

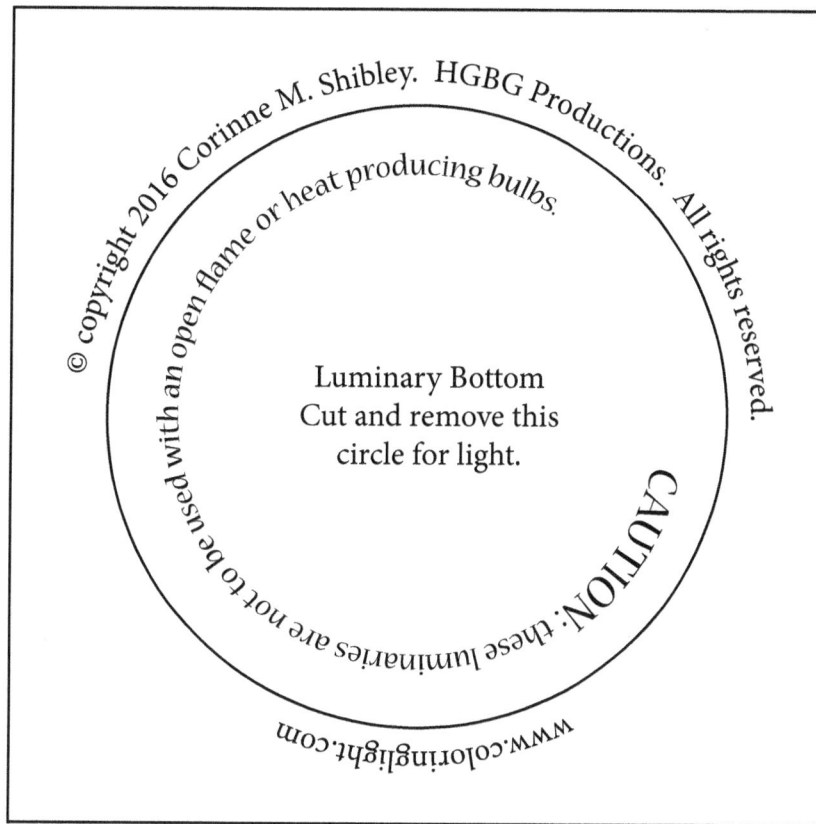

Luminary Top, cut just inside of lines

he rainbow shall be in the cloud,

and I will look on it to remember

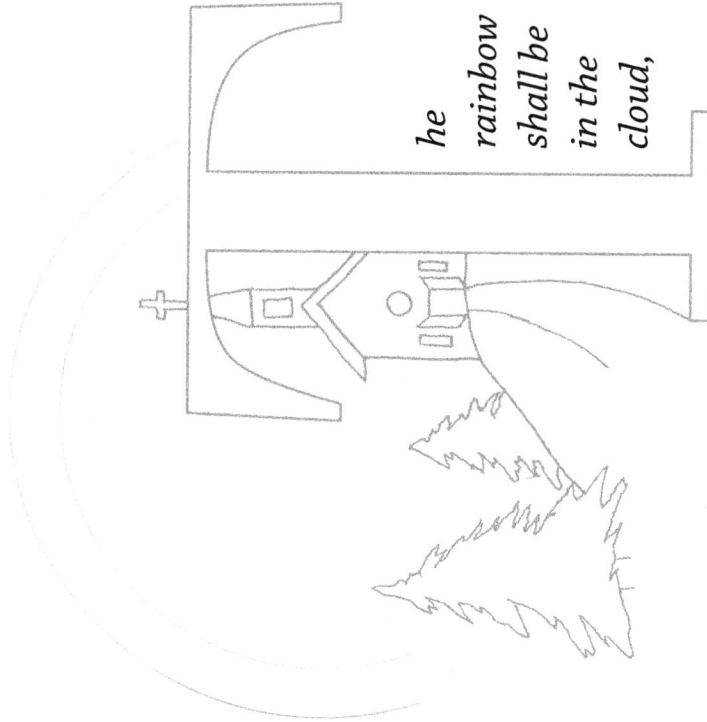

the everlasting covenant between God

and every living creature of all flesh that is on the earth."

Genesis 9:16

© copyright 2016 Corinne M. Shibley. HGBG Productions. All rights reserved.

CAUTION: these luminaries are not to be used with an open flame or heat producing bulbs.

www.coloringlight.com

Luminary Bottom
Cut and remove this
circle for light.

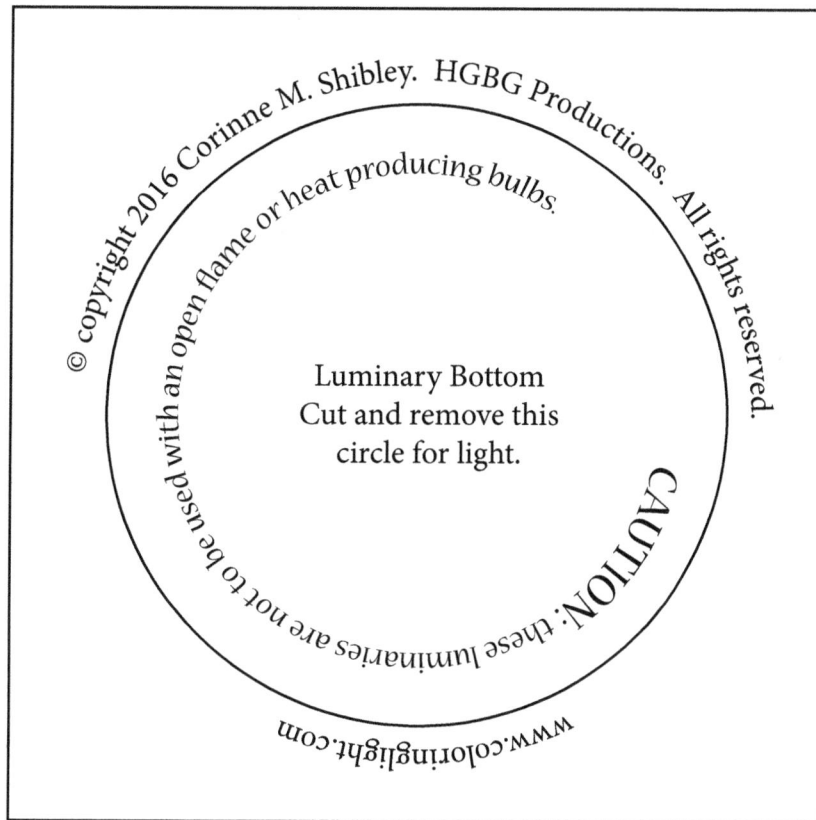

Luminary Top, cut just inside of lines

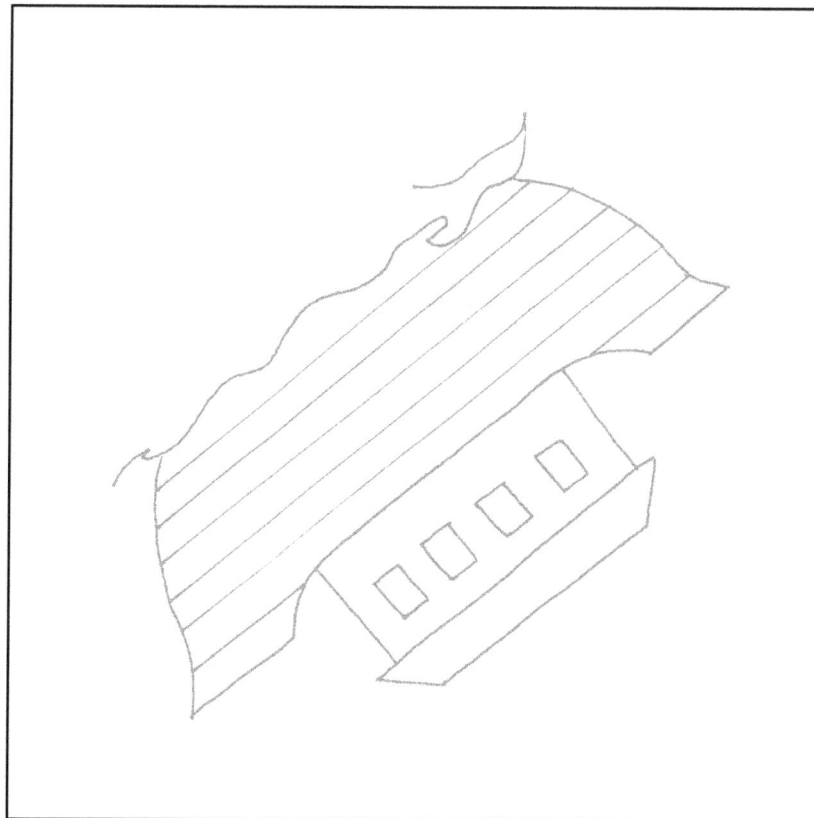

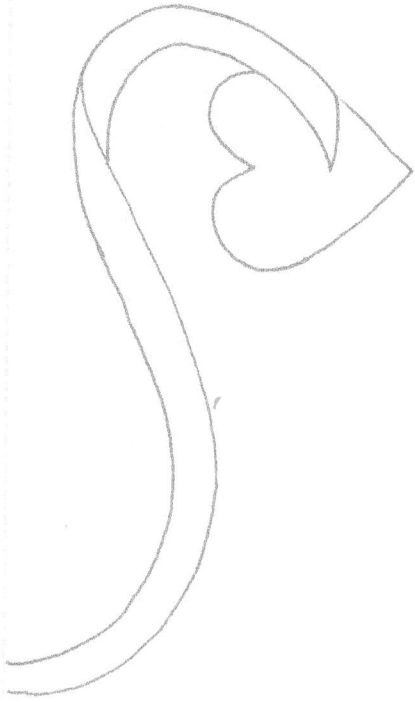

Clearly you are an epistle of Christ, ministered by us,

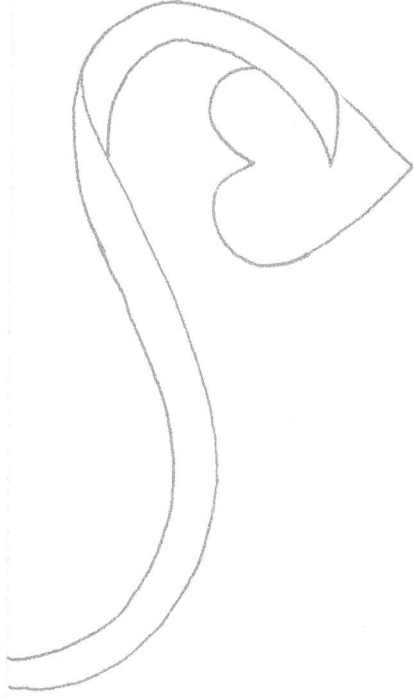

not on tablets of stone but on tablets of flesh,
that is, of the heart.

2 Corinthians:3:3

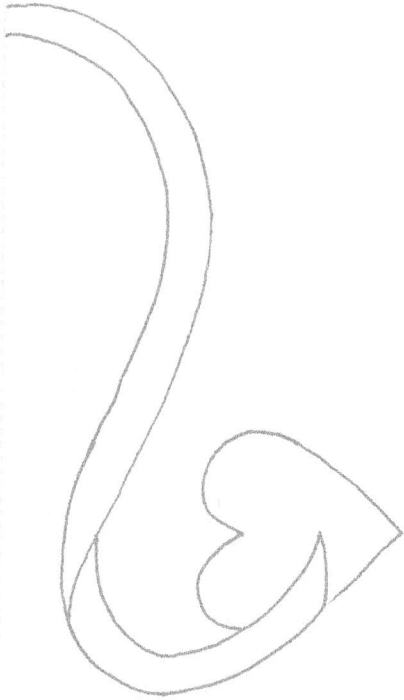

written not with ink but by the Spirit
of the living God,

© copyright 2016 Corinne M. Shibley. HGBG Productions. All rights reserved.

CAUTION: these luminaries are not to be used with an open flame or heat producing bulbs.

www.coloringlight.com

Luminary Bottom
Cut and remove this
circle for light.

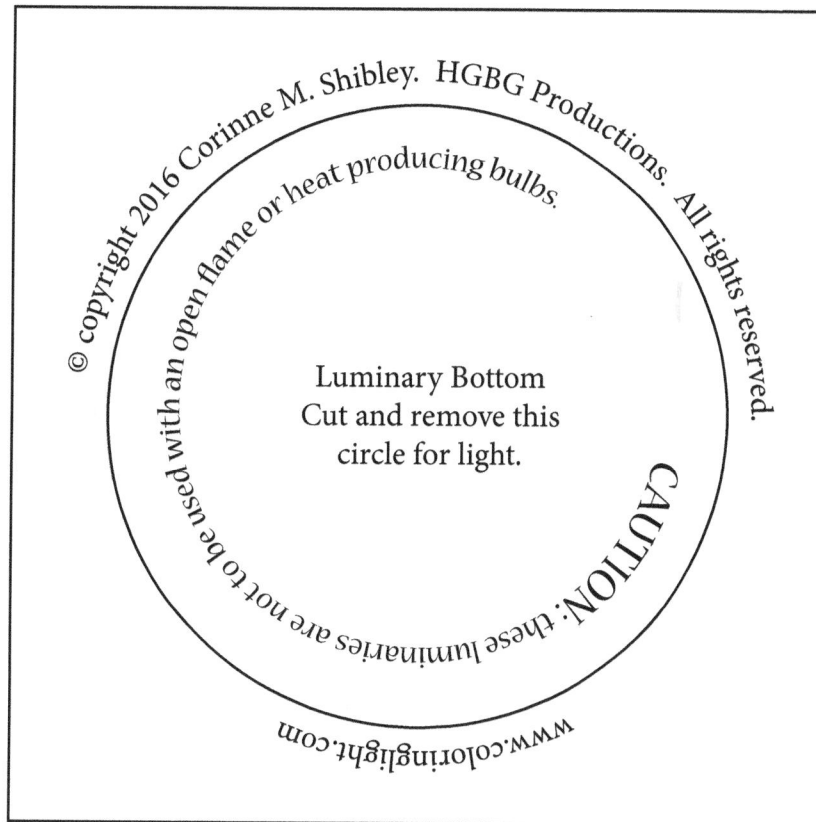

Luminary Top, cut just inside of lines

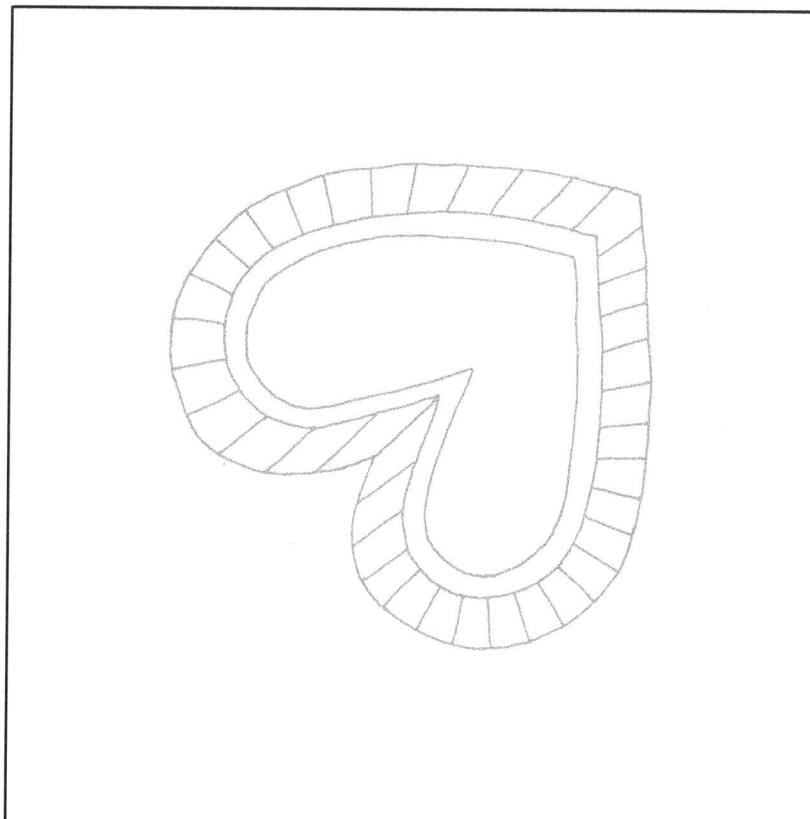

is the beginning of knowledge,

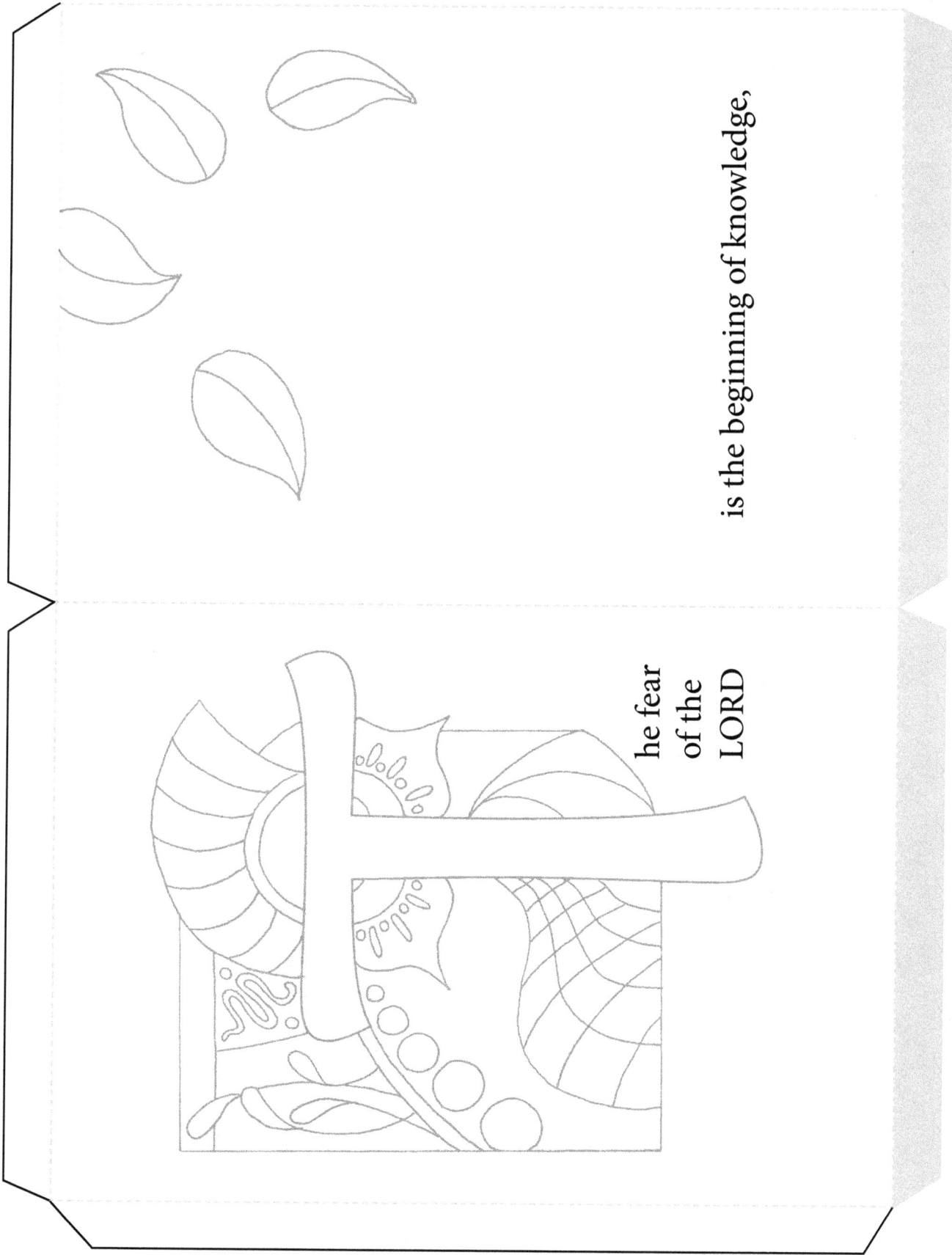

he fear
of the
LORD

and instruction.

Proverbs 1:7

But fools despise wisdom

Luminary Bottom
Cut and remove this
circle for light.

© copyright 2016 Corinne M. Shibley. HGBG Productions. All rights reserved.

CAUTION: these luminaries are not to be used with an open flame or heat producing bulbs.

www.coloringlight.com

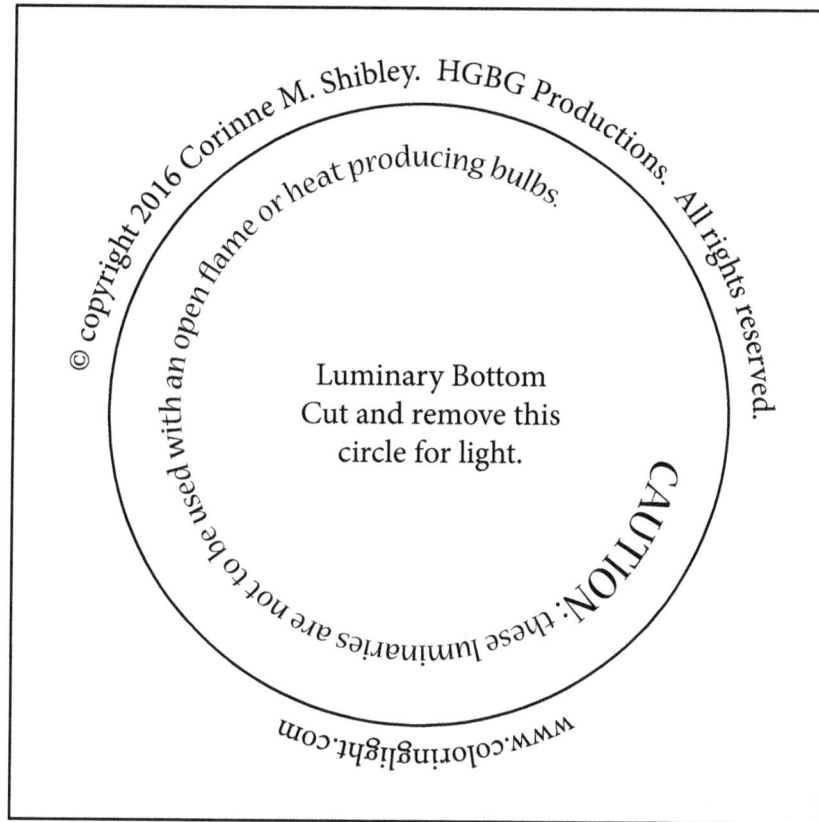

Luminary Top, cut just inside of lines

there is a season,

o everything

under heaven.   *Ecclesiastes 3:1*

A time for every purpose

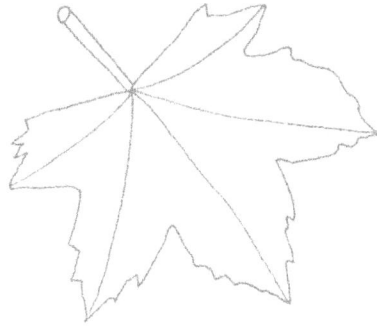

Luminary Bottom
Cut and remove this
circle for light.

© copyright 2016 Corinne M. Shibley. HGBG Productions. All rights reserved.

CAUTION: these luminaries are not to be used with an open flame or heat producing bulbs.

www.coloringlight.com

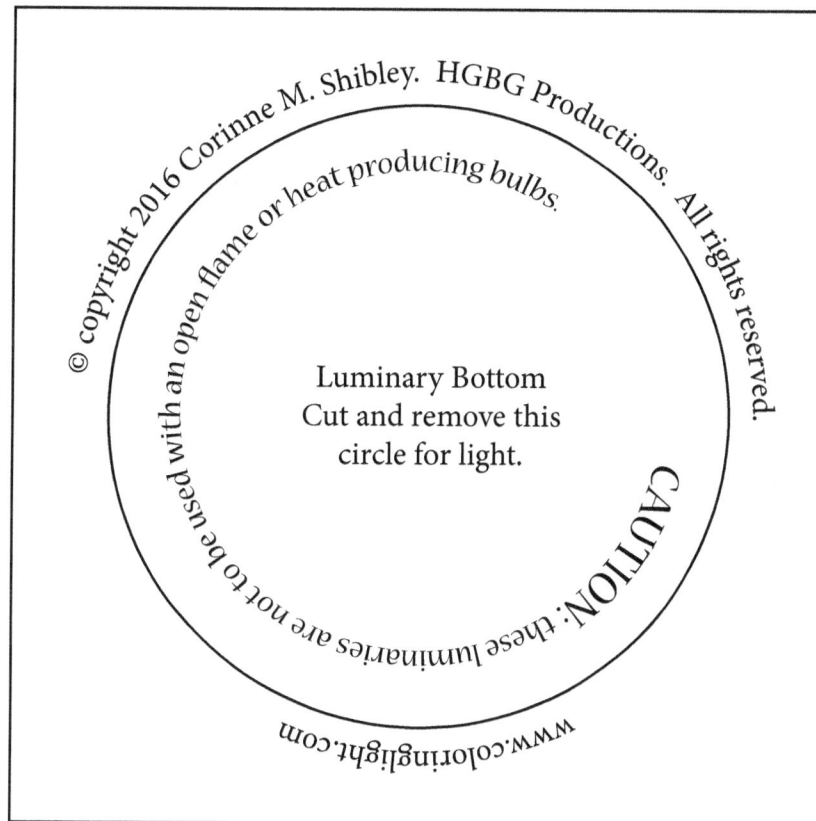

Luminary Top, cut just inside of lines

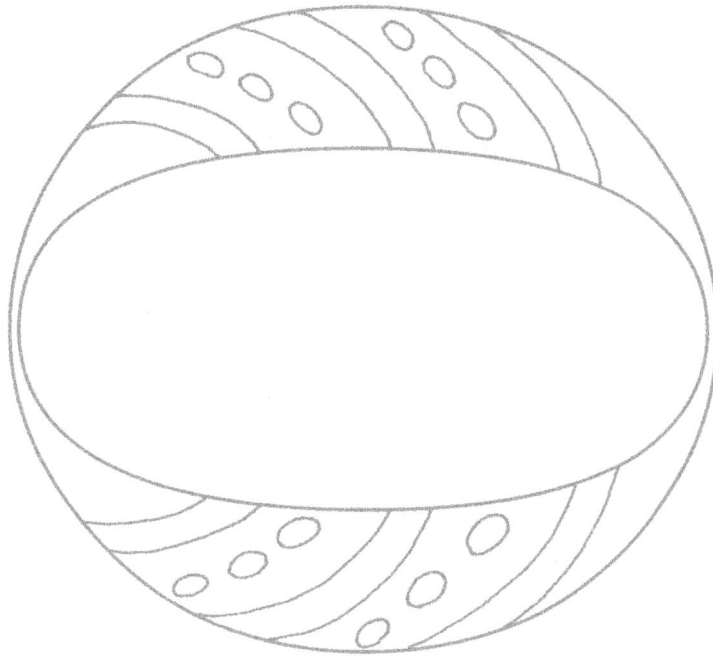

LORD my God, I will give thanks unto thee

for ever.   Psalm 30:12 KJV

© copyright 2016 Corinne M. Shibley. HGBG Productions. All rights reserved.

CAUTION: these luminaries are not to be used with an open flame or heat producing bulbs.

www.coloringlight.com

Luminary Bottom
Cut and remove this
circle for light.

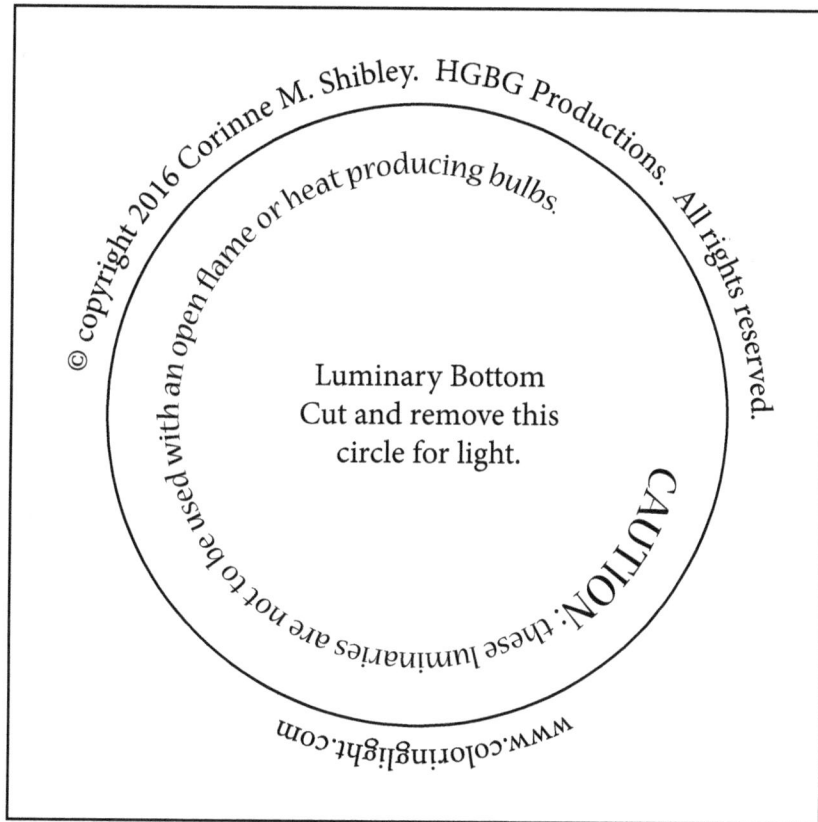

Luminary Top, cut just inside of lines

"For false christs and false prophets will rise

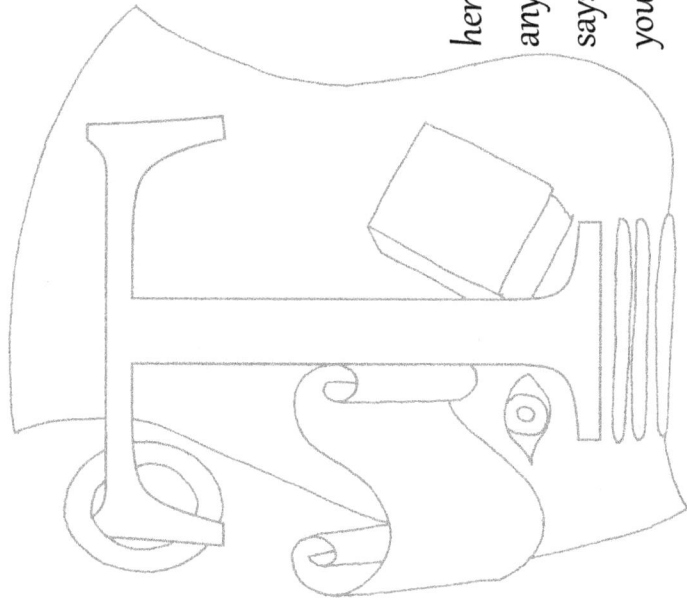

hen if anyone says to you,

'Look, here is the Christ!' or 'There!' do not believe it.

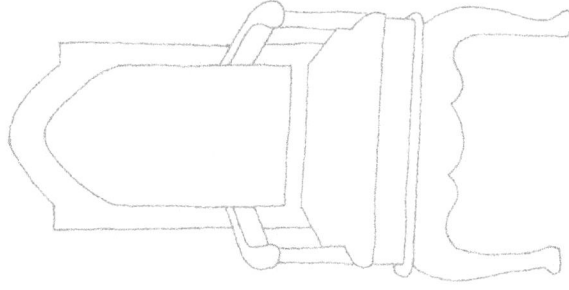

to deceive, if possible, even the elect.

Matthew 24:23-24

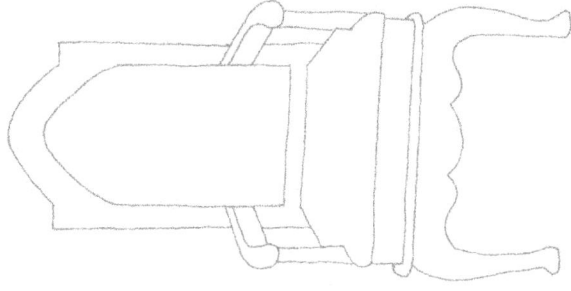

and show great signs and wonders

Luminary Bottom
Cut and remove this
circle for light.

© copyright 2016 Corinne M. Shibley. HGBG Productions. All rights reserved.

CAUTION: these luminaries are not to be used with an open flame or heat producing bulbs.

www.coloringlight.com

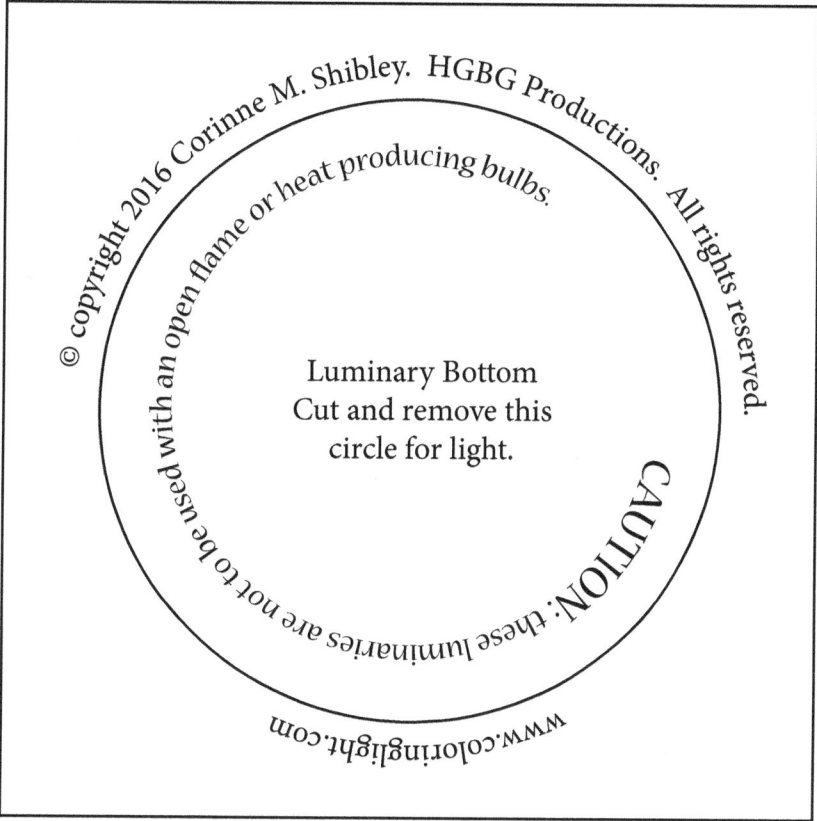

Luminary Top, cut just inside of lines

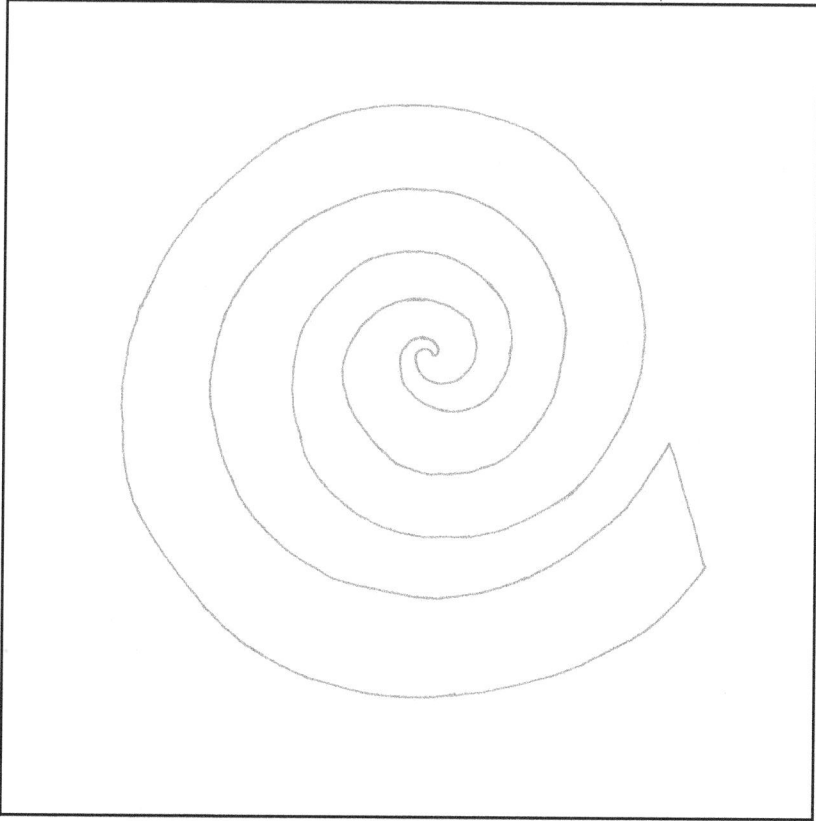

Tips for easy laminating

Clear laminate comes in convenient 12" rolls. Laminate each part of the luminary, front and back, before cutting the pieces. The top and bottom can be laminated as one piece, then cut apart.

Cut 4 pieces of laminate, about 8" x 12". It needs to be smaller than the page, but larger than the finished luminary.

Cut 2 pieces of laminate about 5" x 12" for the page with the top and bottom.

The pieces of laminate will curl, but that won't be a problem.

Peel the backing back about an inch across one short end.

Crease the backing back on itself so there is about an 1" section of adhesive exposed on one end. Without touching the exposed adhesive to anything, and working from the other end, position the laminate over the piece to be laminated, making sure it is totally covered and straight. Press the exposed laminate to the paper.

Slowly press and smooth the laminate as you pull the paper from underneath. It's really very simple, but care needs to be taken to avoid unwanted objects such as hair, crumbs or sweater fuzz sticking to the laminate!

www.ingramcontent.com/pod-product-compliance
Lightning Source LLC
Chambersburg PA
CBHW081540040426
42448CB00015B/3159